THEODORE MARBURG

THE MAN AND HIS WORK

THEODORE MARBURG

THEODORE MARBURG

THE MAN AND HIS WORK

by

HENRY A. ATKINSON

Printed in the United States of America by
Morton Littman Printing Co., Inc.
New York City

To the United Nations

The League is dead! Long live the League! That must be our reply to the repeated assertions, beginning as far back as President Harding's administration, that the League is dead.

It will not die. The need of international cooperation is so great, its advantage so patent, the consequences of its failure so dire, that the world will never again be without it.

Courage, cheerful courage should then be our watchword, while we work and wait. Continue to believe in the world's sanity, in the final triumph of reason and of the ability of men to continue the marvelous progress in organization, national and international, that has marked the past one hundred years. Work and wait!

THEODORE MARBURG

December 1936

Foreword by the Editor

This book has been compiled from newspaper and magazine clippings pasted in chronological order in four large scrapbooks, along with reams of other clippings, manuscripts, letters and records that Mr. Marburg amassed throughout his long and busy life. In addition, the writer has had access to his published works, as well as to those of other authors whose volumes dealt with the problems of these fateful generations.

The editor takes this means of thanking the individuals who have contributed information and incidents and verified dates, and also wishes to thank the following papers and publications for the use of their material:

The Baltimore American	The Washington Post
The Baltimore News	The Christian Science Monitor
The Baltimore Sun	Paris Edition—Daily Mail
Chicago Herald	Syracuse Herald
The Outlook	Paterson Morning Call
New York Sun	The State, Columbia, S. C.
New York Times	Reading Eagle
New York World	Morning News, Waco, Texas
New York Evening Post	The Arbitrator—London
Richmond Times	League of Nations Herald
Philadelphia Press	London Times
Philadelphia Record	Los Angeles Times
The New Commonwealth—London	San Francisco Chronicle
The Washington Star	Atlanta Constitution
The Washington Times	Louisville Courier Journal

No attempt has been made to follow the usual footnote method, except in a few instances. Much of what is written is culled from clippings and other records without the use of quotation marks. The attempt has been made to edit the mass of material into coherent and readable form. Liberal quotations have been made from the following books: *The Development of the League of Nations Idea* (Two Volumes), published by Macmillan & Company; *Bobbylinkapoo* by Theodore Marburg, published by Dorrance & Company; *The Story of a Soul* by Theodore Marburg, published by Dorrance & Company; *In the Hills* by Theodore Marburg, published by G. P. Putnam's Sons; and *Dickens, His Character, Comedy and Career* by Hesketh Pearson, published by Harper & Bros.; *Contemporary Italy* by Count Carlo Sforza, published by E. P. Dutton & Company; *The Story of Woodrow Wilson* by Ruth Cranston, published by Simon & Schuster; *A League to Enforce Peace* by Robert Goldsmith, published by Macmillan Company; *Face to Face with Kaiserism* by James W. Gerard, published by George H. Doran Company; *The League to Enforce Peace* by Ruhl Barlett, published by Chapel Hill Press; *A History of the League of Nations* by John I. Knudson, published by Turner E. Smith & Co., Atlanta, Ga.; *Pioneers for Peace Through Religion* by Charles S. Macfarland, published by Fleming H. Revell Company.

Thanks are extended to Mr. Frank Kent who read the manuscript and made many critical and constructive suggestions; to Miss Ruth Glazier for help in research, especially in the history and background of Maryland and Baltimore; to Miss Louise Congdon, who did a large part of the work in sorting and classifying the material, as well as a major part of typing the first draft of the book; to Miss Irma Scheiber for technical assistance, as well as solving a number of technical difficulties in producing a readable volume; to Miss Hazel Ridout for typing; to Mr. Lawrence Chrow for suggestions, criticism, and technical help; to my associate Dr. A. William Loos for reading the manuscript and making many helpful suggestions; to Mr. F. Grainger Marburg for his careful verification of facts and statements and for his counsel regarding form of presentation; and to Colonel Charles L. Marburg for his cooperation and advice.

HENRY A. ATKINSON

CONTENTS

ILLUSTRATIONS

CHAPTER ONE

The Man and His Background

CHAPTER ONE

The Man and His Background

THEODORE MARBURG was born in Baltimore County, Maryland, July 10, 1862, at a time when the United States was passing through one of its most critical periods. Secession had split the nation, and the war was not going too well for the Government armies. The hopes of the Confederacy to secure support from England or France were wrecked by President Lincoln's dramatic Emancipation Proclamation. This was only one of the many major crises of the 19th Century whose middle years were marked by great advances towards freedom and towards human welfare. This was the age of the Industrial Revolution, with its recognition of the rights of labor and with a new emphasis on human values. In 1847 the "Communist Manifesto" was issued. In 1859 Darwin's monumental work, "The Origin of Species," was published, which led to a long period of unprecedented discussion in schools, colleges, universities and particularly in the churches. Fierce battles between science and religion raged throughout these years.

But it was the year 1848 which marked a real milestone in modern history with its widespread political and social ferments, disturbances, turmoil and revolutions, particularly in Central Europe. The revolution of '48 helped re-establish the Second Republic with Louis Napoleon as president. Three years later he dissolved the Assembly and set up the Second Empire. Italy entered this year into a new era and a brighter future under the leadership of Cavour and Garibaldi. The Prague Conference brought Pan-Slavism to the attention of Europe as one of the determining forces in political affairs. Possibly the most momentous occurrence of that era was the creation of a new German unity through the emergence of Prussia as a dominant power in Europe. Bismarck, the Iron Chancellor, without scruple and with a cynical disregard for either the German people or their neighbors in other countries, forged an almost unbeatable army and navy.

In the train of these events many German citizens migrated to the United States to escape the rising wave of this Prussian militarism, with its arrogance, intolerance, and the brutal methods by which it dominated the nation and its citizens. Among these emigrants was Mr. William A. Marburg, father of Theodore.

The Marburg family traces its origin in unbroken line back to the 13th Century, and to a small estate not far from the city of Marburg which gave them their name. The Marburg family at an early date had split into two branches; one branch, being Catholic, migrated to Austria where its men entered the service of the Hapsburgs and later became Austrian citizens. One of the most distinguished members of this group became a famous general, who received an Austrian county as a reward for his services. It still bears the name of "Marburg," although it is within the borders of present-day Yugoslavia. The Protestant branch of the family remained in Germany. William A. Marburg, grandfather of Theodore, was born in Seigen, Nassau, August 12, 1744, and later became one of Germany's first great iron merchants. Marburg, with its ancient university and its tradition of liberalism, was among the first centers where organized protest arose against the rise of Prussia as a dominating political and growing power. Millions of Germany's best citizens fled during this period, and those who came to America and their descendants have contributed much to our national life.

Theodore Marburg's father was able to come to America with means sufficient to enable him to enter the business life of the community on a fairly large scale. Baltimore in 1848 was already a thriving city and its port famous throughout the world. Soon after arriving in Baltimore, William Marburg met Charles Frederick Munder, who earlier had fled from Stuttgart, Germany, and had already established a new life in Maryland. A close friendship developed between these two men, and within a short time Mr. William Marburg married Mr. Munder's daughter, Christine. There were six sons and two daughters born of this union of the two families. Mr. Marburg, a wise and far-seeing business man, realized that if his fortune was divided into eight parts, only a small inheritance would be received by each of his children. After the Civil War he felt that the Federal Government was strong enough to enforce its excise taxes rigidly and, as a result, he thought an honest tobacco merchant in the United States would have a great future. He therefore purchased a tobacco business for approximately three quarters of a million dollars and presented it to his sons as a joint inheritance, saying that if they made a success of the business they would have many times what would have been their original inheritance had the capital upon his death been divided equally among them. The Marburg Brothers Tobacco Company was bought out in 1889 by the American Tobacco Company for many times the original sum invested. Theodore Marburg, the youngest son, was more interested in intellectual pursuits than in business life, but he took his share of responsibility and did his part in the management of the Company. At the time the business was sold the Marburg brothers agreed that each would serve for a period of at least one additional year as a director of the American Tobacco Company. Theodore lived up to his agreement, but after the year was over he turned aside from business to serious study and research along lines that had become his primary interests.

Theodore was a delicate boy and in his middle teens his older brother William took him on a voyage to Buenos Aires. The voyage was long and the two brothers were the only passengers on the sailing ship. He told many stories and anecdotes connected with the trip, and among his writings we find some allusions; but unfortunately he did not keep a diary and no letters have been found telling of his experiences.

Theodore Marburg attended Princeton Preparatory School, Johns Hopkins University, and Oxford University, England. He was a student at the Free School of Political Science in Paris, and in 1901-1903 attended classes at the University of Heidelberg. This wide range of schooling and travel gave him an interest in social, political, and economic affairs, and laid a broad basis for a life-long interest in international relations. He translated Emile Levasseur's "Elements of Political Economy" from the French and its principles did much to shape a life-long attitude toward public issues. He received many degrees, and from his very earliest days to the end of his life was closely associated with literature, art, science, economics, history, politics and government. The consuming interest of his life, however, was the betterment of international relations, and the substitution of reason and law for the brutality of war.

Mr. Marburg was an enthusiastic horseman. He rode for pleasure, followed the hounds for sport, and as a friend of the family said: "His 'spike team' and fine equipage were as notable as they were noticeable on the streets of Baltimore." He had a genuine love for horses and for nearly every form of sport—particularly for hunting, shooting and fishing. He was a member of a number of fishing and hunting clubs in Maryland and other parts of this country and Canada. He was a good shot, and, as in every other interest, he tried to excel. He felt that it was just as easy to be a good shot as a poor shot; a good fisherman as a poor fisherman; a graceful rider as one who simply sat on his horse. He was also a good driver with a strong wrist instead of a loose-jointed, slipshod hold on the reins.

Among the most fashionable and enjoyable occasions at that period were the party luncheons at the Pimlico Racetrack. These picnic luncheons, or carriage luncheons as they were commonly called, drew large numbers of prominent representatives of Baltimore society. It was on an early autumn morning that young Theodore Marburg, driving his tandem team of well groomed horses, richly caparisoned and hitched to the finest obtainable carriage, arrived at Pimlico to join in the racing events. In a description of these occasions a reporter said, "When Baltimore society goes racing the horses are neglected, for it is 'ladies' day' and these beautiful creatures take precedence." This day was no exception. As Theodore Marburg arrived at the racetrack he found the sun shining brightly, the race enclosure alive with color, the turf green, the track as "attractive" as ever, the blue of the skies above and the trees clothed in their gorgeous late summer foliage shadowing the banks of early autumn flowers in full bloom. It was a day for adventure. Theodore saw and having seen arranged to meet a charming, beautiful, vivacious girl, a belle from Wilmington, North Carolina—Miss Fannie Grainger. He was charmed. Perhaps each was impressed with the other, but certainly he more than she. The writer recently heard the story from Mrs. Theodore Marburg's own lips as she reminisced of that day at Pimlico. She was seated in one of the drawing rooms of the old family mansion where she now lives, surrounded by the beautiful and memorable treasures collected through the long years when she and Mr. Marburg shared their home. She is still beautiful, charming, with a strong sense of humor. When asked her impression of her future husband when she first saw him, she replied with a smile; "On that day when I first saw Theodore I thought he was a pretty fine young fellow, but I was really surprised when just a week later to the very day he visited us in our home in Wilmington. I guess it was love at first sight, for he came the next week; then a week later he showed up again. On that day—just three weeks after I first saw him—we became engaged." Then with a dreamy, far-away look in her eyes, she said, "That was almost exactly sixty-four years ago today." Their life together was a happy one and those years with their wealth of memories remain a constant source of joy.

Mrs. Marburg turned for a moment before I left and said, "I think I ought to tell you that when we came back from our honeymoon we arrived in Baltimore on Saturday evening. Sunday morning Theodore's brother asked me if we were going to church that day. I said we hadn't made up our minds. He said if you do it will be the first time in many years that Theodore has been inside of a church. We did go to church." The fact is that Mr. Marburg, although a member of the Unitarian Church, after his marriage attended the Episcopal Church and became a supporter of its work. He was not effusively nor demonstratively religious, but there was a deep undercurrent of faith and belief in those things for which religion stands. Among his close friends were bishops, pastors, priests, rabbis and other church officials. Cardinal Gibbons was an adviser and frequently a guest in the Marburg home. On one occasion he, together with ex-President Taft, who had just returned from his mission as Governor of the Philippines, met for dinner with Mr. Marburg and considered at length the future of the church and religious life in the Philippine Islands. Mr. Marburg was often called upon to speak in churches and at conferences on religion, and never failed to emphasize the value and absolute necessity of the spiritual and religious approach in solving the world's most pressing problems. The Golden Rule was to him the guiding principle in his life and thinking.

Theodore Marburg and Fannie Grainger were married on November 6, 1889. Four children were born of this marriage: a daughter, Christine Marburg, married to Jonkheer A.W.L. Tjarda van Starkenborgh Stachouwer, who served as Governor General of the Netherlands East Indies for a period before and during World War II, and has recently retired as Ambassador from the Netherlands to Paris. During the war both the Governor

General and Mrs. van Starkenborgh were imprisoned by the Japanese. Capt. Theodore Marburg, Jr., deceased, an R.F.C. pilot with a distinguished record who was wounded in 1915 on combat duty in France; Francis Grainger Marburg, a successful businessman in Baltimore; Colonel Charles Louis Marburg, who served with distinction in the United States Air Forces in the South Western Pacific theatre and also in the North African and East European areas of action in World War II.

Baltimore had in Theodore Marburg a citizen who labored indefatigably for its progress. He was interested in education, art, economics, politics and world relationships. His was a life devoted to unselfish efforts in behalf of his ideals for a better world—free from international disputes, misunderstandings, and war. At the time of his death he was a member of a score or more organizations, working with them enthusiastically and effectively.

His heart was tied to Baltimore, and here he found the greatest delight in his philanthropic work, in pursuing his studies, in delving deep into the economic questions, and in enjoying the society of men, who, like himself, preferred the cloister life to the life of hustle and bustle in the market places of the world.

Baltimore owes much to the Marburg family and is closely related to them and is proud of the relationship. It was said by an English visitor that "Theodore Marburg is the best known Baltimorean in Europe. Dr. William H. Welch was probably better known in scientific circles, but the name of Theodore Marburg was no doubt more frequently on the lips of British, French, Belgians and Germans than any other citizen of Baltimore."

German immigration to Maryland began as early as 1684. These first arrivals were religious mystics and fanatics who were seeking freedom. During the 19th Century Germans came in large numbers, first after the Napoleonic wars when artisans, peasants and businessmen were driven out by bad economic conditions; and again after the suppression of the Revolution of 1848 when political refugees began to pour into Maryland. They influenced the early life of Baltimore and gave it the tradition of religious tolerance, and stimulation of free thought and love of music and order.

The Roman Catholic influence has always been strong in Maryland. Here was established early in the history of the United States a haven for the persecuted Catholics of England, but it did not end with them for the state soon became noted for its liberality and tolerance toward all. Some of the French Acadians who were driven out of Nova Scotia in 1755 settled in Baltimore. The Jews came later and were accorded a free place to live and work and now form an important part of the community. Today there is a remarkable spirit of cordiality, friendliness, and interest in the common welfare on the part of all its citizens. A historian said of Baltimore, "The impulses which created Baltimore were fundamentally moral and physical, 'toleration and tobacco.' The forces which forced her forward were wheat and iron, which found their outlet to the sea through her gates." It was in this city that the Marburg family accumulated its wealth. This wealth was not hoarded, nor spent lavishly for personal and private gratification. Baltimore readily recalls their benefactions.

The Marburg Memorial Building at Johns Hopkins Hospital was made possible by gifts of approximately one million three hundred thousand dollars from the Marburg family. In addition, one hundred forty thousand dollars was donated by Mr. Theodore Marburg and his sister, Miss Amelia Marburg, as a memorial to their brothers, William A. and Charles L. Marburg, to build the Johns Hopkins Faculty Club. A number of important monuments were planned and paid for by Mr. Theodore Marburg, his brothers and sister. A substantial gift was made toward the endowment fund of the Museum of Art; and innumerable gifts to smaller charities totaling several hundred thousand dollars were also provided.

The home of the Marburgs, on the north side of Mount Vernon Place, near Cathedral Street, was a center of refinement, culture and wealth, a magnificent pile of rough marble, the interior arrangements and furnishings of which represented the abode of a man of rare culture and excellent taste. This home has been the scene of many social festivities. Around the dining table have gathered some of the most distinguished men and women of the twentieth century.

Mr. Marburg was interested in maintaining a close relationship and good understanding between the English speaking people of the world. It was at his invitation that Mr. George Haven Putnam of New York and Sir Evelyn Wrench of London, the organizer and creator of the English Speaking Union, came to Baltimore in 1925. He was their host at a luncheon given in the City Club, and here the Maryland Branch of the English Speaking Union was founded. Mr. Marburg was asked to become president, but consistently declined the office. However, he always took an active part in the affairs of the Union. The first president was Dr. William H. Welch, who was succeeded by Dr. John W. Garrett. Later Colonel Charles L. Marburg became president, resigning only last year in favor of the present incumbent. Colonel Marburg still continues to serve as chairman of the board. The interest of the Marburgs in this organization has helped to make it one of the strongest units in the English Speaking Union.

Mr. Marburg was a member of the American Society for Judicial Settlement of International Disputes and many other peace groups. His hopes for peace, however, were not based on "idle dreams," but upon a deep conviction that ultimately the nations can be brought together in a wide organization for peaceful settlement of their disputes. He recognized at the same time the difficulties inherent in the task ahead. He knew that the nations themselves will not and cannot move unless public opinion demands it. His work for peace was for him almost a religion, and the articles of his creed he explained over and over again in newspapers, books, magazines and speeches. These were the three issues he stressed:

First, the establishment of an international court of justice.

Second, the gradual development of the inter-parliamentary union and The Hague Conference into a true world parliament, with an upper and lower house.

Third, the extension of arbitration treaties which will provide that all questions which cannot be resolved by diplomatic methods shall be referred to an international court, no matter whether such disputes involve honor, territory or money.

Through his energetic and stimulating efforts in behalf of world peace, in behalf of peaceful settlement of strikes, in behalf of sound and economic principles and practices in government, Mr. Marburg made a profound and indelible imprint on Baltimore. Through the Municipal Art Society, of which he was the chief spirit, he did much to help beautify the city and to spread imperishable ideas and suggestions for improvements in every department of educational and artistic development.

Mr. Marburg did not practice the arts and wiles of the politician, though deeply versed in diplomacy. His party friends persuaded him to be a candidate for the Republican nomination for mayor in the city political campaign of 1897. His experience at that time convinced him that he was not fitted for a career in local politics and he never again entered that field.

President William Howard Taft on November 22, 1912 appointed Mr. Marburg American Minister to Belgium. He held this post in the diplomatic service for two years and distinguished himself by his services and by the acquaintances he made in both diplomatic and social circles throughout the countries of Central Europe.

Mr. Marburg, while never robust, possessed at the same time a fundamentally sound body and an indomitable will. He was rarely confined to his bed by illness. However, early in 1946 he complained more than usual of weakness and fatigue, but he was not sick enough to give up his activities. He simply slowed down the pace. At the age of eighty-three even the strongest men may be excused for giving into their feelings—but not Theodore Marburg. It was at this time in the spring that he planned a trip to the Pacific Northwest, where he had some property interests on Vancouver Island, and some business interests in the City of Vancouver. He also had a personal interest shared by his cousin, Charles J. Loewen.

When he left Baltimore for Vancouver he announced his intention, after spending several weeks in the north, to go to southern California for a long rest before returning home. He wrote frequently to the family from Vancouver. His letters were cheerful and contained nothing to indicate that his condition was worse than it had been. He died in his sleep on the night of March 3, 1946. His body was brought back to Baltimore, and the funeral services were held at the family home. The honorary pallbearers were: Dr. Matthew Page Andrews, Carlyle Barton, Dr. Isaiah Bowman, Thomas B. Butler, William F. Cochrane, Bruce Cotton, B. Howell Griswold, Jr., Oscar Leser, Dr. Warfield T. Longcope, Dr. J. Hall Pleasants. All of these men were well known in the city and nation.

The *Baltimore Sun* carried this splendid tribute to Mr. Marburg as its lead editorial on March 5, 1946:

Baltimore has got so far from its origins that present-day citizens can hardly be expected to understand without study the special place in the community which was filled by Mr. Theodore Marburg, diplomat and philanthropist, whose death was announced yesterday. Yet Mr. Marburg embodied in his person many aspects of our history and of our hopes.

His family was one of the later representatives of a long series of distinguished German mercantile families who began coming here while the Revolutionary War was still going on. They came to buy for Germany the Maryland tobacco which, under pre-revolutionary law, could be sold only to England. They remained to become pillars of the growing community, to intermarry with its dominant families and to achieve dominance in their own right.

Mr. Marburg was one of the most distinguished and most public-spirited of this admirable group. A man of great gentleness and a special kind of modest but profound culture, he devoted most of his energy and much of his wealth to the furtherance of causes which appealed to him as good. He believed passionately in the practicability of international organization for the maintenance of peace, and wrote and talked on the subject with never-failing optimism. In this cause he became secretary of the American Society for the Judicial Settlement of International Disputes and thus furthered the cause of The Hague Court. The Third American Peace Conference, which met in this city in 1911, was largely the result of his initiative. It charted at least a part of the course which the League of Nations was to take a few years later.

But it was as a public-spirited citizen of the community which had given him birth that he made his more material contributions. The Marburg Building at the Johns Hopkins Hospital is a monument to his family's generosity. The Johns Hopkins Faculty Club, one of the architectural gems of the campus, came into being through similar cooperative effort. Baltimore's magnificent park system grew largely out of his sponsorship of the Municipal Art Society, which had the foresight to bring the Frederick Law Olstead here to study our park needs and plan for their development. His contributions to the Johns Hopkins University, of which he was long a trustee, were generous, even with relation to his means.

Because he was in so many respects a retiring man, a little aloof from the hurly-burly of daily affairs, the generalty of the citizens had little opportunity to judge his achievements. But for those who knew him, he was a man of influence as well as charm. Present-day conditions do not produce many such men. All the more important then to give full recognition to those few who have survived into this generation.

The following resolution was voted by the United Nations Association of Maryland:

With profound regret and personal sorrow we record the death of Theodore Marburg.

A rare soul has passed from our midst. The vision which the prophets revealed—a time of justice and brotherhood among men and nations, the kingdom of God on Earth—is yet to be achieved. Man's progress has been painful and slow. What progress has been made in international understanding has come through the dreams of men and women whose hearts were lifted by prophetic hope.

Such a man was Theodore Marburg. He was among the first of the moderns to recognize that security and peace in our world can be won only as the nations recognize and yield to law. He saw the need for international cooperation and organization as the only assurance of peace among the peoples. With unreserved devotion to our own country he yet possessed the international mind. His was the spirit of the prophet and the soul of a poet. With eloquent voice and pen he pointed the way—forward. He never flinched or faltered. His life and work are inspiration and strength to us to keep faith with him and the hero dead, that justice under law shall unite the nations in the federation of the world.

This resolution, which but inadequately expresses our reverence for Theodore Marburg shall be inscribed upon the permanent record of this organization and a copy shall be sent to the bereaved family, to whom we offer our profound sympathy.

A correspondent to the *London Times* (March 5, 1946) wrote this fitting tribute:

Dr. Theodore Marburg, United States Minister in Brussels from 1912 to 1914, will be mourned by a very wide circle of friends and admirers of his in this country. His name recalls the efforts made in the years immediately after the 1914-18 war to set the League of Nations on its feet. Mr. Marburg was a keen supporter of the League and took a prominent and effective part not only in building up the League movement in his own country but also in helping to establish the International Federation of League of Nations Societies. He was for many years a regular attendant at its conferences—held annually in different European countries—and gave generously to the federation's funds. In these days, when the world more than ever needs men like him, his disinterested work for peace deserves to be remembered.

A saying of the Chinese philosopher Lao-Tse, uttered 2,500 years ago, may be applied to Mr. Theodore Marburg, his work and the influence he left upon the city, the nation and the world:

Since true foundation cannot fail
But holds as good as new,
Many a worshipful son shall hail
A father who lived true.
Realized in one man, fitness has its rise;
Realized in a family, fitness multiplies;
Realized in a village, fitness gathers weight;
Realized in a country, fitness becomes great;
Realized in the world, fitness fills the skies.
And thus the fitness of one man
You find in the family he began,
You find in the village that accrued,
You find in the country that ensued,
You find in the world's whole multitude.

CHAPTER TWO

The Arts, Education, and the City Beautiful

CHAPTER TWO

The Arts, Education, and the City Beautiful

IT WOULD BE DIFFICULT TO FIND a monument or artistic building in Baltimore that was not promoted, at least in some degree, by the generosity and interest of Theodore Marburg and his brothers. He made the proposal for the building of the Art Museum, and the first meeting to discuss the proposition was held in his home.

One of the most attractive memorials is the monument erected to the memory of Francis Scott Key, author of "The Star-Spangled Banner." The statue is the work of the French sculptor, Antonin Mercie of Paris. The foundation and the basin of the fountain were given by the city. The initial gift for this was made by Charles L. Marburg, and upon his death was completed by Theodore Marburg. The dedication ceremonies took place May 15, 1911. As reported in the local press:

> The statue of Francis Scott Key, unveiled yesterday, is one of the most striking and artistic yet erected in this country—a handsome addition to the many statues that have made this the "Monumental City." After music rendered by the Fifth Regiment Band, an address was made by Stuart Symington, Jr. The act of unveiling was then performed by Mrs. William Gilmor, a granddaughter of Francis Scott Key. Little Charles Louis Marburg, the 5-year-old son of Theodore, made his first public appearance and speech as he presented the statue to the city. Mayor Mahool made a short speech accepting the fountain in the name of the city of Baltimore. The various members of the late Mr. Marburg's large family connection and a few specially invited guests were present at the ceremonies, in addition to the many members of the Maryland Institute, the Municipal Art Society and other organizations.

The author of "The Star-Spangled Banner" is depicted standing in the little boat that conveyed him from the British warship on which he was held as a prisoner that eventful night when he watched the shells falling upon Fort McHenry, as he lifts his eyes to the flag that still waves "o'er the land of the free and the home of the brave." The memorial occupies a commanding site, in Eutaw Place, and rises above the lawns and flowers and among the spreading trees of that beautiful boulevard. The sculptor, Mercie, has produced a work that in inspiration and execution is worthy of the author of our national hymn. It is sad to think that the donor, Mr. Charles Marburg, who died before its erection, could not look upon the work of art his munificence has provided. . . .

"The Star-Spangled Banner" was legally designated as our National Anthem by Act of Congress, March 3, 1931. The flag whose "broad stripes and bright stars" Key saw is preserved in the National Museum in Washington. The original manuscript is preserved in the Walters' Art Gallery in Baltimore.

Mr. Marburg was one of the leading members of the Municipal Art Society, which was the first to suggest and map out the proposed civic center. In speaking of it he said:

The development of a civic center need not involve much extra expense. This is particularly true in Baltimore, where we already have three important buildings—the Courthouse, the Postoffice and the City Hall—in proximity. Such a plan means simply proper foresight—that is, providing a location beforehand for new public buildings as they are needed from time to time. If we had had such a plan when the federal government was about to erect the new Custom House, it could certainly have been persuaded to locate the building on the civic center.

When Mr. Marburg left for Belgium in 1912 he loaned to the Maryland Institute Art Galleries thirty of the most important pictures in his collection, which were hung in the Institute's gallery. As reported by the press:

While not extensive, this collection is undoubtedly among the finest art treasures in the South. All of the pictures are worthy of note, and the majority were selected by Mr. Marburg in the course of his travels in Europe. They were not acquired at one time, but are the result of a careful search through the markets of America as well as Europe, extending over a good many years. Intrinsically, the Marburg collection is worth tens of thousands of dollars. The pictures represent some of the best examples of the French, English and American schools, both modern and of earlier date. They have hung in the home of Mr. Marburg, 14 West Mount Vernon Place, adjoining his reception hall, library and dining room, where they have been a source of pleasure to himself and his friends.

Mr. Marburg was anxious to allow the people of Baltimore to see his pictures, so, when he was appointed to his diplomatic post, he suggested that they be displayed in the Maryland Institute. Perhaps the most prominent picture in the collection is a landscape by Constant Tryon (1810-1865), the French landscape and animal painter of the Fontainebleau-Barbison school, who is considered one of the foremost artists of the nineteenth century. Represented in the collection also are Daubigny, Jacque, Moreau de Tours, l'Hermitte, Alma-Tadema, Weiss and Rosseau. Two small pictures by Meissonier are veritable prizes and are exceedingly valuable. Among the pictures held in high esteem by Mr. Marburg are four by C. Y. Turner, the director of the Maryland Institute, including the original sketch of the "Triumph of Manhattan," the mural painted for the Manhattan Hotel, New York. The others are "The Coppersmith," "The Days That Are No More" and "A Puritan."

At the first meeting of the National Society of the Fine Arts

held in Washington, D. C. at the home of Mr. and Mrs. James
Pinchot April 5, 1905, Mr. Marburg, the president of the Municipal Art Society of Baltimore, was the speaker of the evening. Mr.
Marburg began his address by relating an amusing anecdote of a
well-known scholar who, misunderstanding a German noun, insisted that he had no theory of the universe, but sending a rash
guess to his correspondent on a postal card forever persisted in
silence lest his memory failing him, he should not duplicate it. In
the same spirit the speaker declared that he himself had no philosophy of art. To him, he said, it was too big to be reduced to
theories. It meant not, as it is so often misinterpreted, luxury, but
life. Over the fireplace of a Glasgow home of a Scotch economist
he once found the motto, "Not wealth, but life," which he interpreted to mean the fullness rather than the ease of living. With
this fullness he intimately associated art as promoting better ex-
ternal conditions, and the creator of a truly esthetic environment.
"That art marked the degeneracy of a nation," he declared to be
a false premise; "that it developed slowly and was therefore apt to
reach its height late in a nation's lifetime," he said, "was true."
But what is it he continued, "that a nation is remembered by? Is
Greece famous for her commerce? Shall we live on account of our
steel works or cotton factories? And yet art is not an end in itself,
but rather a vehicle. It is not unmoral but rather nonmoral." It is a
mistake, he thought, to hark back too frequently to the art of the
Renaissance and to overlook the strength and virtue of that of the
present day, citing as examples the work of the modern Dutchmen
as compared with that of Rembrandt's contemporaries. The spirit
of the art today, he said, was altruistic—an element unknown to
that of the past ages. Passing to a more definite consideration of
the subject, he made a strong plea for the establishment of city
parks, urging the possibility of purchasing now, as reservations,
plots of ground in the unoccupied suburban districts, and insisting
that by so doing the money expended would bring in the high-

est returns. To the workingman a bit of grass, a patch of sky and well-arranged flower beds were, he declared, more appealing as well as more satisfying, than the best piece of sculpture or the finest painting. What our cities need is variety, and this can only be obtained by wise forethought and cautious planning. As a spur to the energies of the society he pointed out the influence Washington had on the rest of the country; how the example she set, heralded by the press, was followed in other communities. As a concrete instance he cited the mural decorations introduced into public buildings by their use in the Library of Congress and of the smoke law, enforced here, and, in a measure, reproduced in Baltimore. In conclusion Mr. Marburg outlined briefly the career and aims of the Municipal Art Society of Baltimore, organized some years ago with sixty members and now claiming over five hundred. It now has a substantial endowment and its achievements have been many and successful. Great stress has been laid upon the principle of cooperation with the municipality, and the chief effort has been expended on the training and education of the school children—the coming generation. A park system has been laid out and established, notable mural decorations have been placed in the court house, laudable statues in the public squares and other constructive work taken in hand. The problems presented to the Baltimore Art Society were not, perhaps, precisely those which will confront the Watson Society, but their solution was instructive and helpful. Evincing the kindly feeling existing between the sister organizations Mr. Marburg, in the course of his address, made application for life membership in the newly formed National Society.

Mr. Marburg, in an address at Johns Hopkins University, paid a tender but eloquent tribute to Dr. Daniel C. Gilman, who established Johns Hopkins on a scientific basis despite bitter opposition on the part of those who opposed scientific methods. Mr. Marburg said:

To organize in America practically the first true university, destined to contribute by its example to the development of other seats of learning into true universities with aims equally high, is a service of measureless value, a service which must cause Mr. Gilman's name to be dwelt upon lovingly and proudly by anyone who shall hereafter write American history with understanding. What single hand shall trace, in all its ramifications, the influence which Dr. Gilman's work at the Johns Hopkins University has thus had on the intellectual life of the country? But there is a service beyond the service of the intellect. The upbuilding of character is the greatest of all human causes. All of us, no matter how lowly our walk in life, may contribute to it. The clear-eyed and prompt and honest recognition of the just demands upon us of household or community, the decent life, and that first of qualities, the cheerful courage, that does so much to send our neighbor singing on his way, all help the upbuilding of human character.

If this be true of the humblest man and woman and child, how shall we measure the value of such a pure life of service as Dr. Gilman's, so placed as to be seen and known of many men? The sound of his name greets our ears cheerily like the ring of true metal. He has added to the sweetness of life. He has helped men to understand that individual happiness is a true end only in so far as it contributes to the good of all.

We may speculate about immortality, we may have our intuitive convictions about it if you will, convictions that have existed since the beginning of recorded history and before, but of the immortality of the soul we can actually know nothing. On the other hand, the influence that lives on after us, the impress made by our work or by our daily life, the shape that it gives to events by adding to men's knowledge, men's understanding, and, chiefest, to men's purpose, are forces we can know and weigh. In this sense we know that the spirit does live on, that forces set going by one man may spread over millions and take their place permanently as part of the facts of life.

Dr. Gilman's world was a big world. It was rooted deep in history, spread its fibers wide over contemporary life, and will grow green and ample for many a year to come. The Municipal Art Society of Baltimore was in this world of his, one little corner of it, but truly a part of it, because nourished with the same life-giving principle. If its affairs shall be less wisely administered in the future it will be because its officers will miss his sage, suggestive counsel.

Johns Hopkins University was given, at the end of December 1900, a collection of rare and beautiful antiques from the island of Cyprus. The collection includes gold ornaments of exquisite workmanship, engraved stones, seals, and gems of great interest. There are about ninety pieces in the collection, which was gathered by Col. Falkland Warren, a cousin of Mrs. Marburg, who was Government Secretary for Cyprus from 1879 to 1891. Some of the specimens are said to date from 1200 B. C. Professors Archibald H. Sayce and Max O. Richter, the distinguished Orientalists, had examined the antiques and are said to have been eager to secure them for Cambridge University and the Berlin Museum. Some of the relics were purchased from peasants, who had uncovered them in cultivating their fields, while others were secured from excavations made by Col. Warren. The press reported: "This is the most important collection of the kind received of late years by the university. Mr. Marburg, the donor, is a generous friend of the university, and has frequently been mentioned lately as President Gilman's successor."

In introducing Dr. John Quincy Adams, who lectured on "What is Art?" Theodore Marburg gave some of his views on the subject. He said in part:

The prime object of these meetings is entertainment—entertainment of a helpful kind. There is music and there is a good talk ahead of us, something to stimulate the mind and give us a very high form of pleasure—intellectual pleasure. If, incidentally, we get a bit of knowledge with all this, we are by that much the gainers.

It will be a happy result if by this and other evenings together we can awaken a larger interest in art. Art is full of possibilities of pleasure, pleasure of an uplifting kind, like that derived from music. It can hardly be said to make us better men except in so far as it widens our horizon and enables us to see things in a truer light. When it takes the forms of portraying service to men or to the state like the picture of 'Washington Surrendering His Commission' in our Courthouse or the equestrian statue of John Eager Howard in Washington Place, it may of course become a positive force of good.

But there is something to be said for art merely as an educational influence and very much to be said for it as a source of real enjoyment. A very pleasant side of it is that the enjoyment to be derived from it is not a selfish enjoyment. After we have had our mind and our spirit stimulated by a painting portraying in a large way some idea that is of service to men or a graceful monument commemorating a useful life, the object remains for others to enjoy.

The highest modern thought is that the happiness of the individual is justified only in so far as it leads to the general happiness. When a man begins to think of the good of his fellows as his own good, only then is he really fit for rights of any kind, political, civil or social.

To get the fullest enjoyment from art objects we need a little drilling. Everyone who takes up drawing or modeling need not do so with the idea of becoming an artist. The mere acquaintance with form and color gives a new meaning to a picture or a bit of chiseled bronze or carved ivory. Familiarity with land-scape painting lends an added beauty to a country scene in it-self. We seek, and often find, in the landscape in nature the significance and beauty which artists have interpreted into pic-tures with which we are familiar.

Another strong reason for some attention to this subject right here at this particular time is that art is a thing of the mind. Our interests in this great industrial republic are entirely too material. A little acquaintance with art will help us to see that material things are only a means to an end—not an end in themselves.

For the just-minded man the very value of life is not so great as the value of great principles governing the conduct of men. If the interests of the great majority are wholly in one direction, no matter what that direction might be, the people lose a sense of proportion.

Art is one of the many elements of a sound education and education helps me, as the great French thinker, Descartes, put it, 'to conquer myself rather than fortune'—to change my de-sires rather than the order of the world, and generally to accus-tom myself to believe that nothing is so entirely within our power as our thoughts.

It has been said that "an artist is a person who lives at the very center of life itself and tries to see it as a whole, while a prophet lives outside and looks at things from the periphery of existence." Like all generalizations, these are not wholly true for the real artist has in him some prophetic qualities and every prophet of any significance also has some attributes of the artist. The artist "accepts things as he sees them." The prophet "sees things as they ought to be." According to these definitions Mr. Marburg was an artist, a poet, and a prophet. He probably had some of the love of "art for art's sake," but in most things he reflected the great ideals which originated in Ancient Greece. Real beauty, he thought, must be more than mere line, form and color. The word "character," which basically means beauty, carries with it the ideas and ideals of moral excellence and ethical values. Mr. Marburg in many of his speeches, and particularly in his letters, showed a great impatience with the slowness of progress toward a better and a fuller life for the individual and the world. So, we must conclude that while he was a prophet as well as an artist, no one would think of him fitting the cynical definition of a prophet as "a frustrated man of action." Most of the critical situations he saw emerging were faced boldly by suggested practical plans to meet them. He "cried aloud" to his generation, and "viewed with alarm" certain evils developing within the framework of our democracy. Nonetheless, he lived so close to the center of life that he not only raised his voice, but he put his shoulder to the wheel and did his utmost to help cure the ills he feared.

Perhaps the best example of his real interest in and love for art is expressed in this speech he made as chairman of the Joint Committee of the Municipal Arts Society and the State Commission, having in charge the responsibility for the adornment of the beautiful Maryland Courthouse. The occasion was the unveiling of the picture of Washington Bidding Farewell to His Troops. The address of Mr. Theodore Marburg in delivering the picture into the custody of the city through Mayor Hayes was of a most interesting character. Mr. Marburg not alone dwelt upon the great artistic merit of the composite, and upon the need of stimulating a love of art among the people, but gave a highly interesting sketch of Mr. Edwin H. Blashfield, the eminent artist of New York, a painter of mural decorations.

The address, in part, was as follows:

The decoration which the joint committee of the Municipal Art Society and the Courthouse Commission is turning over today to you, Mr. Mayor, as the representative of the City of Baltimore, is but a feature added to the beauty and dignity of a fine building. It was because the architects had in mind just such noble adornment as this that it is possible for us to place it here. The painter works to disadvantage unless the architect has consciously provided opportunity for him. Such opportunity is not lacking for making the Baltimore Courthouse one of the noted buildings of the world. We start with pure and beautiful lines of architecture and find within the Courthouse spaces for a series of decorations which it might well take many years to provide. Our painter, Blashfield, brings his tribute in these words: 'The dignified restraint shown in the interior architecture of the Courthouse is particularly helpful and even inspiring to a mural painter, who feels that such handsome rooms demand very serious decorative treatment.'

The decoration which Edwin H. Blashfield has given us here touches a high theme in the world of politics. How many leaders, inspired by enlightened patriotism at the beginning of their career have marred their work by proving incapable of resisting the temptations of power? How different our destiny and that of many other lands whose course has been influenced by our own had Washington proved equally weak.

The act which this painting portrays illustrates pre-eminently this moral strength of the man. It was the crowning act of devotion to the cause that owed so much to him. The event occurred on December 23, 1783. Washington had asked Congress, in session at Annapolis, whether it desired him to tender his resignation in writing or in person. Congress expressed a preference for the latter course. The committee of arrangements for the day was composed of Jefferson of Virginia; Gerry, of Massachusetts, and McHenry, of Maryland. State and government officials thronged the house, and many ladies were present.

Members remained in their seats with hats on, after the fashion of the mother country; others stood uncovered. The tall figure of Washington wore its usual air of dignity and composure as he delivered the short address conveying his resignation as commander-in-chief of the Army. The president of Congress replied and the ceremony was at an end.

We will come to realize, if we do not now realize, that Blashfield has pictured this great event in a great way. He has preferred to touch it with allegory rather than transcribe the actual scene. The decoration is admittedly one of the best productions of this eminent painter, and the Baltimore Courthouse will be known to an additional number of men as the home of Blashfield's Washington.

CHAPTER THREE

The Poet and Playwright

CHAPTER THREE

The Poet and Playwright

In ADDITION TO HIS public services Theodore Marburg was a writer of no mean ability and was well known and highly regarded as a poet and playwright. One of his publications, "In the Hills," is a small book of verse containing not more than a dozen poems all told. They are not such as to commend themselves to admirers of ultra modern verse, for they are clear in meaning, rhythmical in language, didactic and frankly emotional in the old style at times. That, however, commends them to most readers, as will the fact that they are sincere, thoughtful and imaginative. A prose poem, "Follow the Flag," recalls, in these days of disillusionment to many, the ardor with which America entered World War I. If the high hopes of world peace are ever fulfilled it will be because of the flame that has burned and is burning in the hearts of men like Theodore Marburg.

FOLLOW THE FLAG

FOLLOW THE FLAG!

By every fireside where live the love of country and the love of justice is heard a sigh of relief that our flag is not, after all, to be trampled in the mire. Now that it has been raised aloft, follow it! Follow it even to the battle front.

FOLLOW THE FLAG!

It goes on a *high* mission. The land over which it flies inherited its spirit of freedom from a race which had practiced liberty for a thousand years. And the daughter paid back the debt to the mother. Her successful practice of free institutions caused the civic stature of the citizen in the motherland to grow. It lit the torch of liberty in France. Then, moving abreast, these three lands of democracy imparted to it impetus so resistless that freedom is sweeping victorious round the globe. Today constitutional government is the rule, not the exception, in the world. Once more these three nations are together leading a great cause and this time as brothers in arms.

FOLLOW THE FLAG!

It goes on a *world* mission. If the high hope of our President is fulfilled, that flag will have new meaning. Just as the stars and stripes in it symbolized the union of free states in America, so now they may come to symbolize the beginnings of a union of nations, self-governing, and because they are self-governing, making for good will and justice.

FOLLOW THE FLAG!

It goes on a stern mission. Follow it, not for revenge, yet in anger —righteous anger against the bloody crew who, with criminal intent, have brought upon the world the greatest sum of human misery it has ever known in all its history. Follow it till that ugly company is put down and the very people themselves whom they so grievously deceived and misled, by coming into liberty, will come to bless that flag and kiss its gleaming folds.

FOLLOW THE FLAG!

Too long it has been absent from that line in France, where once again an Attila has been stopped. It has been needed there, God knows! And yet, though not visible to the eye, it is and has been there from the beginning. It is there in the hearts of fifty thousand American boys who saw their duty clear and moved up to it. Now at last it may be flung to the breeze in the front line, to be visible by day, and to remain at nightfall, like the blessings of a prayer fulfilled, in the consciousness of men. Follow it and take your stand beside the fifty thousand.

FOLLOW THE FLAG!

HAVE YOU FORGOTTEN?

Ye little souls, who think America
Can fiddle while old Europe burns, where is
Your memory, where your understanding?
Have ye forgotten how America
For months leaned backward in a vain attempt
To hold herself aloof when that disaster
Of the ages, the World War, was bringing
Death to millions?
Your ilk said then 'Tis no
Concern of ours if predatory nations,
Out for plunder and for blood, attack
Their fellow nations cross the seas.'
Have ye forgotten how our nationals were done
To death in peaceful passage of the seas?
Have ye forgotten, too, the aftermath
Of war, the mortal and material
Collapse, the business blight and tragedy
Of unemployment, bringing universal
Woe to neutrals and belligerents
Alike? Must we not then take risks for peace?
Can ye not see that should America
Courageously declare today her purpose
To employ her military might
Against aggressors who may seek again
To follow bloody paths, there will be peace,
Long peace in Europe?

A poem called "Perugia," printed in *The Independent,* February 1915, attracted considerable attention. This poem follows the rhythm and meter of Tennyson's "Locksley Hall." Here is an historical retrospect in which the spirit that guided Raphael and St. Francis of Assisi, "Love of God and love of beauty, beauty of the mind and soul," is held up as the true inspiration of life. There are touches of symbolism here and there, and underneath an all-pervading optimism.

Selected verses from "Perugia"

On thy hilltop, bold Perugia, with the shadows flying o'er
All the tangled vine and olive lying round thy ancient door,

Circled by thy ring of mountains capped with cloud or winter
    snow
Thou dost gaze in contemplation on the happy fields below.

Far beneath thee flows the Tiber singing of the ancient deed,
How it washed the Pagan temple ere the birth of Christian creed.

Memories of thy rude beginnings, older than the Roman sway,
When thy bold chiefs swept the valley, red and ruthless birds of
    prey;

Memories of the Middle Ages—when again rough might made
    right—
Of thy freedom stoutly guarded on the castellated height;

How, when gentler manners triumphed, thou didst turn thy
    thoughts to art,
Playing in that great awakening not a mean nor trivial part.

For thee Perugino labored in a deep religious mood,
Passing on the spark of purpose to his youthful painter brood.

And among them stood the Raphael, caught the master's fire and
    skill,
Saw the visions that were destined all the after years to fill.

Men still study him and love him in all lands where art hath place.
So dost thou, his teacher, linger in the memory of the race.

Yonder gleaming on the hillside sits Assisi old and grey,
Still the shadow and the sunshine on its lofty spire at play.

Seems the order Francis founded seven centuries ago
Stable as the rock he sleeps on in the mystic crypt below.

Each new generation knows him, knows his war on greed and pelf,
Knows the positive upbuilding and the mastery of self,

How he put aside his fortune, hand in hand walked with the poor
Ministering to mind and body, bringing hope to many a door.

From the time that human motive first began its upward flight,
When the mind of man still slumbered darker than the starless
        night,

Dreams have come of life hereafter, nay, conviction that the pain
Of the earthly dust and travail surely have not been in vain.

Lending richness to the present, stealing, from the unknown fear,
Making labor of the spirit growth and culture all more dear,

Even offering consolation in the bare and sterile ways
Where uninteresting labor brings no hope of better days.

In the far-off lonely cabin and among the city's throng
Lulled to sleep is human sorrow by this olden cradle song.

Yet we know not, yet we know not if the cherished hope be true
All pervading and enduring through its iridescent hue.

This we know: that man has purpose, God-inspired but still his
        own,
Will to climb, to plan, to venture, will to conquer the unknown;

Know the iron in his spirit holding him with steady zeal
Faithful to the seen and unseen, tho' they break him on the wheel.

Human will made history. Let man take the praise and blame—
So will failure of his duty mantle still his cheek with shame—

In the clash of human interests offer but one prayer at night;
For the strength to do His bidding which is strength to do the
    right;
One fear only in his bosom; wholesome fear of doing wrong—
'Tis the fear of God in substance making men and nations strong.
Cheerful courage ever marking all the progress of the day,
That which helps to send our neighbor singing on his upward way,
If His purpose be in all things, progress of the race we hail
Through an ever higher conscience to a will that shall prevail.

JOIN HANDS

(This poem was first delivered at a luncheon of the Maryland Branch, League of Nations Association, at Baltimore, on January 29, 1935.)

I

Join hands, Columbia, with thy sister nations!
Sustaining hands of fellowship await thee.
Ominous the ever-darkening shadows!
Now as never all the nations need
The help of each. Thou, my country needest
Them no less than they need thee.
Join hands.

II

A century and a half ago, the light
Of morning on thy countenance,
God flung
Into thy lap great fundamental laws
As broad and wise as men had ever known.
Nobility of soul was thine, high courage
And high purpose; steadfast aim to point

The way to larger government of self.
He cradled thee within a lovely land
And gave to thee great opportunity.
Hard work, hard thinking was thy lot with vast
Reward. Midway down the century
A fearful ordeal tried thy soul.
Came with it
Stalwart men who helped thee to survive.

III

Swept down upon a breathless world, next came
That darkest hour of human history,
The unbelievable, the fateful assault;
Triumph of unreason just when perception
Of the horror and stupidity
Of war had grown apace in Western lands,
Europe was aflame and liberty
And justice stretched out bleeding hands to thee.
How vain the effort then to stand aside!
When once aroused, two million sons of thine
Poured o'er the seas to right the awful wrong.

IV

Havoc threatens once again. In one
Direction only lies the certainty
Of peace. Be one, my country, with the world
In fearless, full responsibility
For peace, and peace will then be undisturbed.
Join hands!

A final poem—

COMPENSATION

When every glistening blade of grass
    And every thirsting flower
Are drinking deep the blessed drops
    Left by the passing shower;

When every sorrow bravely borne
    And trials of the heart and mind
Bring resignation to His will
    And knowledge more refined;

When sore defeat in what we sought
    Turns out our lasting gain,
Revealing higher guidance than
    The powers of the brain.

BOBBYLINKAPOO

When this poetic story first appeared the critics compared it to parts of "Through the Looking Glass" and Mr. Marburg to Lewis Carroll who, in his leisure time from teaching mathematics, wrote fantastic and attractive stories. Mr. Marburg wrote this small but delightful book, one suspects, primarily for the pleasure of his own children. "Bobbylinkapoo," a story of child adventure in an elfin atmosphere of make-believe, written in swinging and lilting measure, is filled with the rare magic of fancy and imagination. And what a heart of beauty he displays in this enchanting poem!

An Indian boy of tiny size was Bobbylinkapoo,
With bow and spear and tomahawk and beaded buckskins too.
Though e'er so small and full of mirth he'd lived for many a
    year
A sort of wonder person to the Indians far and near.

And every Indian loved this lad and every tribe was gay
When soaring on his eagle, he would set his course their way.

Their Little Chieftain he was called; they knew him as a brave
Whom neither cold nor hunger stayed, nor black bear in his
cave.

'Tis the hour beloved of the fairy world and presently to the ear
Come the strains of lovely music, soft, but very sweet and clear;

And, glancing above, they see them dance around the magnolia
bloom
With flashes of moonlight from their wings against the deep
tree's gloom.

The moon that had queened it in the heaven all night
seems loath to settle to rest
'Mid the broken clouds, still silver-tipped, on the
rim of the world in the west,

As if she would linger to rival her lord who has
not as yet appeared
But who throws back his head and laughs at the
thought till they see his flaming beard.

At the age of seventy-six Mr. Marburg wrote his first play—
"The Story of a Soul"—which was produced two years later at
the Baltimore Museum of Art by the Johns Hopkins Playshop.

The play, a poetic tragedy, details the brief but dramatic career of the young and beautiful Marie Adelaide, who ascended
the throne of the Grand Duchy of Luxemburg in 1912, the year
in which Mr. Marburg assumed his post as United States Minister
to Belgium. In 1919 the French government forced Marie's abdication, charging that she had violated neutrality by entertaining
Kaiser Wilhelm at dinner and by being seen, with her sister, in

the company of officers of the German Army. Broken hearted, the young sovereign entered an Italian nunnery and died several years later at the age of thirty. Her closest friends in her exile were her lady-in-waiting, Countess Montgelas, who remained faithful to the end, and Prince Xavier Bourbon Parma, whose marriage proposal Marie rejected.

As a statesman Mr. Marburg was able to observe this tragic history at first hand, and he also knew many of the principals and their families personally. He met Marie at The Hague and had intimate friends in the Bourbon Parma family.

In translating the story of Marie into blank verse, Mr. Marburg received guidance from Edith Shaughnessy's biography of the Grand Duchess, and from research in the Library of Congress at Washington. There he gained authentic material from the official proceedings of the Belgian Assembly. Marie's abdication speech in "The Story of a Soul" is translated verbatim from the original, which was in French.

When Mr. Marburg completed the play in 1938 he submitted it through the United States Ambassador at Brussels to the court of Marie's sister, the Arch Duchess Charlotte, then ruler of Luxemburg, for approval. "The court has no objection to anything so beautiful," was the reply.

The following striking tribute from the late Grand Duchess Marie Adelaide's homeland appeared in the Luxemburg WORT, November 26, 1938:

Just as there are things in the physical world which the rashest of us venture to touch only with the lightest of fingers, so there exists personalities in life in the presence of whose spiritual greatness and tenderness of soul even the most boisterous are silent.

It is not so much the appeal to the heart that impresses the sensitive person when he explores the destiny of such an one, but rather the mysterious element of fate, that resistless power of the tragic, revealed in Aeschylus and Sophocles and to a lesser extent in the words of all true dramatists.

Yet, the deepest and stillest personalities are often buried in oblivion. In the burial ground there has long rested an extra-ordinary personality, a woman to whose speeches we hearkened and who was once the radiant embodiment of our nation, Marie Adelaide. Facing overwhelming difficulties, she was mastered by a fate such as few heroines or heroes in the greatest masterpieces of all literature have suffered.

Foreign lands could not forget this queenly woman as easily as her homeland. Abroad several most intelligent writers have sought out and set forth the facts concerning the life of our noble Grand Duchess. In the usual manner of biographers, they limit their account of her more or less to the events of her life and her death, without taking the pains to explore the under-lying elements of tragedy with which the dramatist deals. No poet of the homeland has as yet undertaken the fruitful task of laying before us the greatness of this contemporary tragedy in drama form for the stage.

But a work has come to us from the United States which bears quite simply the profound title 'The Story of a Soul,' its author Theodore Marburg. If we are not mistaken, the poet, who is much esteemed in his own country, was formerly Amer-ican Minister to Belgium and therefore well acquainted with all the happenings in Luxemburg. The drama is lyrical throughout and overflows everywhere with feeling and outgivings of the heart and spirit.

The author has sought to set forth the leading events in the life of our first Grand Duchess in order to reveal, in a number of beautiful passages, profound and full of feeling, the outward and inward graces of this wonderful woman. In part his metre has a swing which carries one away. Especially where he lets Marie Adelaide speak, he clothes the soulful utterances in surprisingly sweeping phrases, a quality which in fact characterizes all the monologues and dialogues and gives to them the worth and power of surpassingly beautiful poetry. Listen simply to the revealing of the young soul in the first act:

> I like to be alone.
> One sees alone the things one cannot see
> In company.
>   They wonder why I stay
> Away so oft from family prayer and linger
> So much in the church's door instead of
> Entering in to share the common worship.
> It is because I find myself made rebel
> By the constant preaching of the fear
> Of God and frightful future punishment.
> To me, left in the open air, with all
> The mystic beauty of the world about me,
> There can be no such thing as fear of God.
> For God is love. What men mistakenly
> Call fear of God is fear of doing wrong.
> The love of God is love of right.'

> Although we know it to be
> Blessed release from suffering, yet when
> The dark, forbidding angel beckons those
> Whom we hold dear and pushes wide the door,
> That door through which we all must some day pass,
> How trying the vast emptiness they leave!
> There is a knowable world which God permits us

To behold and, yes! increasingly
To understand. And close beside it lies
Another world our understanding is
Unequal to and ever will be.
Let my faith reach far beyond my understanding.
The soul itself must be the citadel.
Direction's everything and distance nothing.

There are many such moving and soulful passages in which
unalloyed pathos rings. They cause the greatness and the purity
of the soul that has gone home to reveal themselves and this the
more wonderful because they are simply the poetic rendering
of true and historically authentic characteristics. For this reason especially we recommend this work to our people. Moreover, it has appeared opportunely on the eve of the centenary
celebration of the founding of our worthy dynasty. It fills one
with sadness to see how soon a people can either forget or show
themselves too sluggish to correct, even partly, a wrong of yesterday. A friend said to me recently, 'Marie Adelaide is a Lux-
emburger, perhaps one of the greatest Luxemburgers of the
recent past. And yet she lies buried in a foreign land.' In connection with our centenary celebration, would it not be most
becoming to lay her, with due ceremony, in the princely vault
here? Would not such an act be exceptionally symbolic and
impressive?

This is a challenge to the patriot. Another challenge is that
to our home poets. Cannot one of them create for us, for our
home festival and in our native tongue, this great home
drama?

CHAPTER FOUR

Economics and Social Progress

CHAPTER FOUR

Economics and Social Progress

IN NEARLY ALL OF Mr. Marburg's letters and speeches he presented the moral and ethical considerations of government and economics as well as the principle of expediency.

His viewpoint was in great measure shaped by the writings of Pierre Lavasseur as we have stated in the first chapter of this book. He was influenced also by the theories advocated in the writings of Diderot, Voltaire and Jean-Jacques Rousseau, all of whom had urged reason as a substitute for prejudice, tradition, dogmatism and conventional goodness. Voltaire, for one, had protested against the cruelty, inequality and injustice of the economic and political systems of France. His faith, which was shared by his compatriots, was based upon a rationalism which struck the spark that became a glowing flame which, spreading, led to the revolution in the English colonies in America.

Thomas Jefferson, Thomas Paine and others, who were awakened to action by the concepts of these great thinkers, incorporated many of the teachings of the French philosophers into the American Declaration of Independence. Principles which had been conceived as applicable only to France were now accepted as universal.

In the following pages no attempt has been made to cover the entire range of Mr. Marburg's interests in governmental and economic affairs. However sufficient examples are quoted to illustrate his attitude toward such issues as "Governmental Interference"; "The World's Money Problems"; "Panics"; "Shorter Hours of Labour"; "Taxation" and "Municipal Ownership." It is to be noted that many of Mr. Marburg's economic theories seem to be outdated; at the same time many of his suggestions have been enacted into law, such as the control of the railroads by the Interstate Commerce Commission; the Sherman Act; guarantee by government of bank deposits and other similar legislation.

GOVERNMENTAL INTERFERENCE

At a certain period of our development, liberty came to mean freedom from restraint by the State for the reason that the State in the person of arbitrary rulers had been an oppressor. At that juncture it was highly important to take a stand against State interference in order to correct abuses. But when this was successfully accomplished, the fight for liberty was by no means won; only the first stage of it was won. The struggle had now to be directed against the oppression arising outside the sphere of the States, that is, against certain institutions or customs, which give to corporations and individuals the power to oppress others. When the State has been won over to the side of the people and is administered by and for them it at once becomes possible to increase the liberty of the average citizen by having the State interfere with certain practices, old or new, which curtail that liberty.

The logical basis of State interference is the assumption that the unconscious evolution which prevails in the animal world becomes partly conscious and self-directed evolution when we reach man, who thinks. This process is greatly assisted by democratic institutions, under which the people act more as a single organism. The united thinking of the many serves to develop a sense which no individual enjoys. The world will never be able to do without leaders. Progress will still be ordered by the few. But the significant thing is the growing ability of the masses to choose between contending ideas and contending leaders.

If natural selection, which means the killing off of the unfit,

were relied upon alone to modify ideas, false beliefs and practices could disappear only with the disappearance of the people
holding and observing them. In human affairs, the conscious
element, reflection, spares the race this hardship.

Human institutions have as their object the bringing into
play of natural laws which are beneficial, and the avoidance of
acts which natural laws show us to be harmful. The institution
of the school is based directly upon this principle. With education, the man becomes the heir of all the past, the inheritor of
the strivings of the human soul in the fields of conduct, of religion, of art, of imaginative literature; the sacrifice made for
fellowmen in a bygone era is made again for him since knowledge of it stiffens his courage and purpose; what these prophets
have seen and these heroes have done, he can see and do; the
larger purposes of the world shine out through all its tangled
and painful happenings; that thing, more real than the solid
globe itself, the will of man, is seen in its true light as the moving force of history.

If men grow up in ignorance of the past; if they are not
taught to use this tool civilization, which assumes so many
forms in mind and matter, they are apt to run counter to natural laws and suffer unnecessary hardships. The State recognizes
this fact and proceeds to interfere with the liberty of the parent
by compelling the parent to send the child to school. The institution of the church serves the double purpose of upholding
the moral code which saves men from mutual destruction, and
of implanting ideals which operate as a positive force.

There are several reasons why we should move cautiously in
the matter. In the first place, it becomes difficult, in the course
of time, to judge whether the State is conducting a particular
enterprise economically. Data for just comparison is lacking.

Moreover, people do not examine critically the cost of State service. If there be a deficit, it is covered in the general budget, the claim being made that the people are getting the service at less than cost. Again, are we likely to have as rapid progress in a given industry under State ownership? . . . .

But even were economy of management and progress not at stake, there is yet an element of grave danger in this movement. I mean the evil which arises from multiplying the number of public servants.

This class lives upon the State and may sap its very life. We must not forget that when we take such a step, it is not for today and tomorrow but for the long future. Turn over the street railways, with their army of 140,000 employees, to the municipalities and, presently, a demand will arise that the steam railways be acquired by the State or Federal government. Some unwise practices on the part of other services would precipitate a demand for their acquisition. That road leads to abolition of private property and to socialism.

The penalties of mismanagement of enterprises owned but not operated by the government will be principally economic while government operation, involving an important increase in the number of government functionaries, may work serious injury to our institutions, the evil of the one being temporary; of the other, permanent and fundamental.

Regulation of the charges of public service corporations is a well established principle but, there again, the question of expediency may, at any time, be raised. Are we not, for example, attacking the wrong end of the railway problem when we attempt to fix rates? Two great sources of railway accidents and casualties today are the single track and grade crossings. The single track is a source of freight congestion in time of business activity. Would it not be wiser to compel the railways, by law, to lay double tracks and to abolish grade crossings; to give us frequent and speedy service; in other words, to benefit themselves while they benefit us, rather than for us to pursue a policy which will reduce railway earnings and, thereby, postpone the advent of needed improvements? Ought we not to leave the railways profitable, speculatively profitable, if you will, because of there being few greater factors in the progress of the country than railway extension and improvements?

To fix a limit to the activities of the State by setting up a Code of natural rights, with which the State must not interfere or to determine the field of the State's activities from an analysis of the nature of the State, is simply to becloud the various issues which confront us from time to time. It is better to separate the two. The State is empowered by law to do many things which the dictates of expediency cause it, in ordinary times, to refrain from doing. On the other hand, if we arrive at the conclusion that a certain course of action is socially expedient, we can set about amending statutes and constitutions where necessary.

As has been cleverly said, compulsory vaccination may be based on definite data but 'theological experts can produce no similarly trustworthy statistics about the relation between orthodoxy and immunity from damnation.'

The unrestrained play of private interests, similar to that of national rivalries, does not always make for justice and, in so far as this is true, State interference rests upon common ground with all human law.

Objections, valid against State interference when a prince and his favorites can impose their will upon the people, no longer obtain when the people make their own laws.

When the State prohibits to the railroads grade crossings; when it proscribes for them patent couplers and block signals; when for factories it institutes boiler inspection and demands that dangerous machinery be guarded and unsanitary conditions corrected, it is restricting the liberty of individuals or small groups of individuals while, at the same time, it is increasing the liberty of many times their number. State interference, in the modern sense, may raise the ceiling of the poor man's cabin and enable him to stand upright.

When it is proposed that the State should regulate the hours of labor for adults or compel parents to send their children to school, it is frequently argued that men have a right to work as many hours as they like, as well as the right to send their children to work.

But the idea that the individual has certain natural rights, of which the State cannot deprive him, is passing away. Men are beginning to realize that all social right resolves itself into social expediency, that is, the ultimate welfare of society in the long result. The doctrine of natural rights served its purpose in the day when tyranny often took the form of harmful interference with the free action of the individual. Instead of following this circuitous path, we now appeal directly to social expediency. Whatever it is expedient that the State should do, it has a right to do. Right in this sense is, of course, something different from legal right which is determined by law. The State now deprives the criminal of the foremost of his so-called natural rights, the right of life. It forbids us now to do certain work on Sunday. If it thinks it socially expedient that it limit the hours of labor on week days and forbids child labor, it has a right to do so.

If this reasoning be correct, the only limit that can be placed upon State activity is the limit which the facts of the past and of the contemporary world prescribe. These facts, however, must be weighed in the light of the capacity, tradition and the present condition of each particular people.

It is an error to start with any preconceived notions either for or against State interference. *The end of State action, as we have seen, is to enable the individual to realize himself more fully in the State.* In the case of specific measures, it has been suggested that we ask: First, does the end proposed lead toward our ultimate end? Second, are the means adequate? Third, are they too costly?

THE WORLD'S MONEY PROBLEMS

This speech, made by Mr. Marburg in 1896, at a meeting of the National Civic Federation in New York, is of interest to us today, at a time when, in spite of the Fort Knox gold, our exalted favorable balance of trade has caused an unfavorable imbalance of economics throughout the rest of the world. This impasse threatens, in turn, to react disruptively on our own economic system.

It is curious what a far-reaching effect the money supply of the world has upon its well-being. Just before the discovery of America, the lack of precious metals brought untold evils, social, political and economic, upon the whole of Europe. The quantity which America shortly afterwards supplied caused a tide of prosperity which had such an important result as to hasten the fall of the feudal system. Poverty had kept the people down but when the new life, which America sent them in the form of a new money supply, began to course through their veins, the stature of man straightened and the rotten fetters of the feudal system began to snap. In France, in the course of the following century, that type of landholding relationship rapidly disintegrated until, in the time of Richelieu, it ceased to exist as a political system.

In the present century, before the discovery of gold in California, the world was feeling keenly the scarcity of money metals, this despite the bimetallism prevailing on the continent of Europe which enabled France, for example, without abandoning her monetary system, to let England and other countries have nearly all of her gold. In 1838, only five per cent. of her circulation, including the reserves in the Bank of France, were in gold.

The yield of gold in the fifties brought needed relief and great prosperity. For England, a gold currency country, it was very timely indeed since, according to some authorities, it stimulated, to the point of saving, her commercial prosperity. So, again, the recent South African discoveries (1896) are as water to the thirsting. The disasters we have suffered this time, owing to causes which are now plain, are of such magnitude as to constitute a new experience.

The secret of our dependence on the supply of the money metals is that an ample supply of sound money stimulates industry. After all, it is the continual employment of human hands and heads which gives the world its wealth. In order to appreciate this, one need only consider how large a factor in the cost of production are wages and to apply this to a specific case, such as railway construction. Here, the greater part of the expense is wages paid for making and laying the road. Before the completion of a railway, the amount thus disbursed in wages has nearly all been consumed in the maintenance of the laborer; only a small percentage has gone into the savings bank and become capital. The significant thing is that these men must continue to consume, whether in a useful occupation or not. As a result, in times of business activity we have such an industry as a railway in return for a given amount of food and clothing for the laborers while, in hard times, we have a large proportion of this amount consumed without getting anything in return. This fact leads one to believe that the evil effects of a great business depression can be somewhat lessened, even permanent results secured, if the government, at such times, embarked on a liberal public works program.

To recognize any such thing as a right to employment is impracticable and, to attempt it, by offering work to all the unemployed would be disastrous. It would inevitably draw recruits to the ranks of the unemployed by taking away from men the necessity to maintain themselves in private industry. The principle is not that. It has nothing to do with sentiment. It is simply what reason would dictate, namely, that it is better to turn idle men, who must continue to consume, to some useful work, thereby leaving to our children a worthy public monument, in the nature of a road or bridge or noble building, than to permit consumption to go on without any return. With the advent of better times, such work would be discontinued as speedily as possible in order not to interfere with normal industrial conditions.

We must bear in mind the improvement in the people's standard of living if we are to fully appreciate the increase in the demand for money. Just as the renaissance is now remembered for its revival of letters and the Age of Pericles for its intellectual brilliancy, our century will probably live in history as a result of its inventions. These have brought about an enormous increase both in consumption and in trade in a multiplied population in which the needs of each individual have multiplied. This is why the money basis is still short, notwithstanding the great increase in the production of gold.

The assumption that the use of credit supplants the need for money to the full extent of the credit is unsound. Every credit is really a credit of material wealth and can be brought into play only through the medium of money. If a cotton manufacturer borrows ten thousand dollars with which to buy cotton, although the transaction is made through a bank credit, it is the cotton which the lender is making available to the borrower for a certain length of time. All such credits are, at bottom, based upon money. If the currency of the country in which such a transaction takes place has a gold or silver basis, it is the actual amount of gold or silver in the banks or in the government vaults on which the credit must ultimately depend. In addition to the metallic reserve as a basis for credits is the fact that, in retail trade, there is generally an actual passing of money. The needs of an advanced civilization call for a great increase in the supply of money. This is amply illustrated by contemporary facts, even within the boundaries of a single country.

PANICS

There have been so many disastrous financial panics in the United States, as well as in other countries, that many people have come to believe more implicitly in economic charts, which depict when the next "boom" or "bust" may be expected, than in the essential soundness of our economic and political systems. Even now, there are prophets who are reading the signs of disaster on every hand, the more pessimistic of whom are saying that the next depression, followed by a panic, will mark the end of the present monetary standard. Mr. Marburg was one of those who refused to accept this theory. Speaking before a meeting of the American Academy of Political and Social Science in Philadelphia April 10, 1908, at a most critical moment of the panic, he said:

It is safer and more helpful not to accept too freely the fatalistic theory of periodicity of panics but, instead, to look for the special cause of each panic. Accumulating experience should enable us to prolong the interval between, eventually preventing entirely the recurrence of panics—just as epidemics of disease, formerly thought inevitable, are now prevented.

In connection with the panic of 1907, it is difficult to discover any widespread speculation or overproduction. However, we do know that, for five years previous to the panic, we witnessed a shrinkage in the market value of many leading railroad securities in the face of increased earnings.

This panic was largely centered in the United States and, therefore, it is necessary to seek local causes. Chief among these appear the attitude of the federal and state governments toward the railroads and, next, the extravagant fine on a single industrial trust. Together, these occurrences have left the investing public uncertain as to the value of two vast classes of securities.

The remedy for the abuse of industrial trusts probably lies in the direction of federal control through license. The moment corporations are required to register under a federal statute, whereby the government may require certain information of them, the possibility of great reform at orce appears. When attended by publicity, compulsory investigation into illegal and unjust practices tends not only to correct illegal practices but the unjust practices as well, without resort to proceedings in a court of law or even in a court of arbitration. Possibly nothing except the knowledge that these corporations can be controlled by the federal government, and are being controlled by it, will stop the popular attacks on them. And what applies to the industrial trusts in this connection applies equally to the railroads although, here, the federal government might possibly go a step further and resort to actual incorporation of interstate railroads under federal law, as distinguished from the mere licensing of industrial trusts. It may find it wise and even necessary to do more than control the practices of the rail-roads, that is, to interfere with their actual operation by insisting on improvements of the service. Of course, if the government assumes such a position, railroad earnings must not be interfered with.

Another potent cause of the panic, a cause which has been generally recognized, is the inelasticity of the currency. The problem of an emergency currency revolves principally around the question of what constitutes an adequate tax on such currency. Without an adequate tax, the currency will not contract sufficiently in normal times and will, therefore, lack proper elasticity in anormal times. Furthermore, without such tax, there is serious danger that inferior money will take the place of good money. Two things conjointly cause gold to be drawn to a country. One is the providing of a place for gold in the currency system of the country, the other is the interest rate.

The crisis of 1907 was aggravated by a run on the banks. Two devices suggest themselves as calculated to prevent a recurrence of this: One, postal savings banks, the advantages of which must be apparent to every student of public questions; the other, a guarantee by the federal government of deposits in national banks. It would be a distinct gain if, while having a secure currency, we could, at the same time, make secure the deposits in national banks. This guarantee could be made without risk of financial loss to the government if a small tax were imposed on the banks, the proceeds of which would constitute a guarantee fund, along with the government being empowered to levy an extra assessment on all the national banks, in addition to the regular tax whenever the guarantee fund fell below a specific amount fixed by the statute.

In view of the panic of 1929 and the desperate years that followed, the panic of 1907 now seems like a very small affair. However, Mr. Marburg's analyses are just as pertinent to the greater as to the smaller recession in business and general welfare. Mr. Marburg makes several concrete suggestions on methods of avoiding panics. Since the great economic and financial collapse in 1929, which began almost simultaneously in Europe, Australia and in this country, we have passed a number of new laws in the United States for control of the banks and the development of a sounder and saner foundation for our economy. The principles enunciated by Mr. Marburg are sound and, while we cannot be certain that our system of bank credit and control will weather every possible storm, Mr. Marburg's thinking in world terms at least indicated his faith in national and international control as a solution for most of our problems.

SHORTER HOURS OF LABOR

In 1902, when the movement for the shortening of hours for labor was being bitterly fought by industrial interests, Mr. Marburg gave a lecture at Johns Hopkins University on December sixth, which disclosed his views on the problem.

Few of us doubt that the unexampled economic activity, upon which our country has entered, points to ascendency in the field of industry. What concerns us is the study of the forces that are calculated to make our position secure and enduring. There is reason to believe that the cycles of growth and decay that mark the history of nations were born of conditions that are being modified. Those regions of the earth which, because of cultivation, have become centers of human activity, are rapidly filling up. Even we shall probably not escape the fate of other nations, except for postponing the day of decline while hoping to show some lasting gain to humanity as a result of our activities. That latter object can be promoted best by building up the character of the average man in the United

States. To effect this, we must give attention to the labor question and to the ethical side of industry.

We need as a perspective a consciousness not only of the contribution of machinery to wealth, but of the part it has played in bringing about greater opportunities for employment, as well as higher wages. The great increase in the number of people who follow gainful pursuits, not only in Europe but in America —where the phenomenon is explained partly by the existence of new land to be cultivated—has taken place since the advent of power machines. In the United States, money wages have advanced 82 per cent, and real wages 130 per cent, since 1840. There is no question but that machinery is synonymous with increased opportunity and increased wages.

The increase of wages is bound to come to the laborer, even though he has not concerned himself with securing it. If it does not come in the form of an increase in money wages, it comes as cheaper commodities which, in reality, represent an increase of real wages. However, improved conditions of labor, including the lightening of the task, do not evolve so automatically. Here, the free play of economic forces has failed to produce the desired results.

Adequate leisure for the laborer will do more for society than a further increase of wages. Thus the progress of industry, in the past, justifies the hope of further progress since the legitimate object of the movement for shorter hours may be the diverting of the benefits of such progress from the channel of increased wages to that of increased leisure.

It might be urged that it matters little whether industry gives away the increase in the form of wages or in the form of leisure. Nevertheless, such an assertion needs to be qualified. If the gain goes to the laborer as increased pay in money wages or real wages, it increases the purchasing power of this class and stimulates industry. For the moment, industry would gain more by the increase in wages. But the true interests of society are best subserved by increasing the mental, moral and physical stature of the workingman. In this respect, the interests of both industry and society are identical.

In the long run, because of competition with other employers, no single employer can make a radical reduction of hours. The same is true of any single State of the Union. It would be dangerous for any one State to limit hours in the general field of industry much below the average in other States. However, in non-competitive industries, such as the telephone, telegraph, gas and electric lighting, street railways, retail shops and everything which partakes of the nature of local service, the State can insist with safety on shorter hours independently of the action of other States.

States and municipalities, in granting franchises, may make the hours of labor a condition of the grant. It is seldom that municipalities make a proper charge for franchises. Therefore, such a provision is not likely to cause franchises to go a-begging.

In the general field of industry, any movement for a reduction of hours must be by trades or by action of the Federal Government, a matter which, with respect to the latter, would require a change of the Constitution.

On the part of particular trades, a movement is already on foot to bring about shorter hours through concerted action. As to the individual employer, he demands that he be placed on an equal footing with his competitor, home and foreign. Recently, the National Civic Federation sent out a number of inquiries to employers in certain trades, asking them whether they were willing to concede a shorter working day in consideration of the laborer abandoning his practice of limiting output. Sixty per cent of the replies were favorable.

However, any reduction of hours must be made gradually through a period of years, just as our industries grew under the Clay-Calhoun compromise which reduced the tariff 5 per cent a year through a period of nine years. This gradual reduction, without a doubt, acted as a stimulus to invention.

Following these arguments for shorter hours, Mr. Marburg in a subsequent article dealt with the relation of a labor government to international control. He said:

I suggest that one specific change in our Constitution which is urgent is provision for social security legislation by the State and national governments. If the dislocation of labor, due to invention and better organization in various fields, is to be tempered, we need ever higher wages to absorb the increased product and ever shorter hours to absorb the surplus labor.

But here again, we must see the matter whole. Can these benefits to labor be systematically maintained here unless the leading industrial countries of the world practice them at the same time? A pact made through the International Labor Organization at Geneva, of which our nation is a member is indispensable. Such a pact is possible provided it is agreed to quota, or exclude entirely, the products of countries refusing to adhere. The two measures are interdependent, the treaty and the constitutional amendment which would make it possible for the United States to live up to the obligations of the treaty. It goes without saying that this cannot be done in a day. But, if it is the only way to deal successfully with the problem of employment, we should make up our minds about it and at once take initial steps looking to the realization of the double program.

TAXATION

Quoted from a pamphlet by Mr. Marburg (1898).

The income tax is a just tax. We must find, sooner or later, a way of again introducing it here in America despite the decision of our Supreme Court which has pronounced it unconstitutional. Income is the real measure of what a man should contribute toward the public revenue. In some countries, when one speaks of what a man is worth, this does not refer as much to his property as it does to the income from his property. There is nothing in the constitution of many of our states to prevent those states from collecting income taxes. The danger lies in driving capital from the particular state which imposes the tax. We are, therefore, forced to turn more and more to our central government, as in this case, for the solution of pressing questions.

The greatest need for revenue today is in our municipalities. The federal government readily collects what it needs and the finances of most of the states are as easily managed. It is in the cities where more each year is necessarily being spent on public health, safety, education and comfort that revenue is needed. It is a question whether the requisite, increased amounts needed can be gained from the sources tapped by taxation at present. New sources will probably have to be considered and one of the most obvious will naturally be incomes. In no way can incomes be reached so successfully as through the central government. Therefore, by following this method, each state and municipality would receive back its proper quota of the sum collected. We should find here a large and growing source of revenue, as well as a method which the taxpayer would ultimately recognize as equitable.

Another very just source of revenue is the inheritance tax,

especially since a liberal tax of this nature imposes less hardship on a community than an income tax. As to a tax on personal property, the difficulties met with in attempting to collect such a tax remain, and must remain, insurmountable. Vast amounts of such property, however, are now being reached in another way. Many enterprises which were formerly private concerns are now taking the form of corporations and issuing stock. The moment this happens there is something tangible for the taxing power to lay hold of. The corporation pays the tax and the stockholder receives his dividend, less the tax. In Baltimore, the great corporations, such as the street railways, gas company, banks and financial trust companies pay taxes in this manner, as do, in fact, industrial corporations. The holder of the stock cannot escape the tax because his income, from such investments, is taxed at its source.

After the income tax and the inheritance tax, a tax on luxuries, considered solely as a tax, and not, like the tariff, as a means of promoting industry, is probably the most just and least injurious of taxes. Tobacco, wine, beer and spirits are things which men can do without. Those of us who insist upon having them may, therefore, be properly called upon to contribute liberally toward the necessary expense of government. Such a tax may either be in the form of duty on an imported article or of an internal tax, or as a high license upon local traffic in the article. Certain nations of the world collect very high revenues from tobacco, wine, beer and spirits. In some countries, where the manufacture of tobacco is a government monopoly, the state enjoys the profit of the enterprise as well as the tax collected.

With us, the tax upon luxuries principally takes the form of an internal revenue tax, a tax on an article manufactured within the country. In this instance, there is no doubt as to the person who ultimately pays the tax. None of it falls on the manufacturer, nor on the wholesale dealer—it is paid by the consumer. A marked advantage of this system is its flexibility. The tax may be raised or lowered, according to the needs of the government, without any disturbance to industry worth mentioning. It is interesting to contrast this with the business paralysis which ensues from the mere agitation of a change in tariff rates.

On the subject of taxing franchises, Mr. Marburg said:

What we should look for from public service corporations is, first, the quality of the service; second, the cost of the service, and, last, the public revenue. An example of this is the street railways. We want, first of all, frequent service and rapid service; then, and next in importance, we are concerned with the cost of the service—the fare. A rapid service and a low fare bring social benefits which are difficult to overestimate. When the railways of Baltimore adopted rapid transit, they did more for the comfort of the people of Baltimore than any one event since the introduction of gas for lighting. No action of the municipal government in its sphere could possibly have added so much to the comfort and welfare of the people. But the emphasis laid on the quality of the service. The cost of the service included a proper consideration of the question of public revenue from franchises. In all such instances, sufficient profits should be left to make the enterprise highly attractive but, over and above this, the whole of the revenue should really go into the public coffers. One way to accomplish this is to grant a franchise for a limited term of years, so that it may be revalued and sold to the highest responsible bidder at stated intervals. Such a system of revaluation, honestly carried out, would tend to prevent overcapitalization which is, at present, one of the greatest wrongs commonly inflicted upon the public by public-service corporations.

A second method for securing for a city a proper return for franchises is by taxing the franchise annually like other property, the market value of the stock being used as a basis for ascertaining the value of the franchise. Still another is for a city to share the profits of the enterprise after a certain maximum dividend is paid to the shareholders.

MUNICIPAL OWNERSHIP

Quoted from pamphlet written by Mr. Marburg (1899).

The consideration of public attitude toward public corporations, together with the ultimate effect of such organizations upon the community, involves the question of state or municipal ownership. This question, which is being agitated in many places both in America and in England, calls for as serious attention as any problem before us. If we are wise, we will make haste slowly in the direction of lessening private initiative in any sphere of activity in America. There was a time, when a cleaner administration was needed, that I rather leaned toward municipal ownership as a thing to be desired. But I have found myself gradually undergoing a decided change of attitude. Now, I have reached the definite conclusion that for us in America extensive state undertakings (the term includes municipal undertakings) would be a misfortune. Although it is not a question of the ability of the state to conduct these services economically and effectively, even here we must discriminate between the services which it might take over. For example, no one questions today the advantages resulting from each city controlling its own water supply.

A city which has a clean and efficient administration could

probably save money by taking over a service in which, for example, there remain few problems to be solved, such as the supply of gas. On the other hand, lighting by electricity is so new that our cities, had they gone into that business a few years ago, would have been the losers. In fact, there are still so many problems unsolved in regard to this service that, even today, if our municipalities were to take over such an enterprise, they would interfere with the progress which is promised for the industry under private initiative. Suppose, for example, that the street railways throughout America and in the leading cities in Europe had been owned by the municipalities when the cars were still being drawn by horses. Do any of us believe that public action would have been as enlightened as private initiative has been in introducing rapid transit? Is it not likely that many cities would still have a service entirely of horse cars? Even so, the evil I have in mind is of another kind, an evil more serious than the evil of delay. It is the evil which arises from multiplying the number of public employees under a democratic form of government.

As we read these addresses and articles we realize that Mr. Marburg foresaw and forecast many of the issues that were current in his day. No one will agree with all his opinions, but the matters that attracted his attention and the issues that he discussed are the same ones that are demanding our attention at present, and which in the years that lie ahead must be grappled with by our people, our Government and the world at large.

Politics

CHAPTER FIVE

Politics

THE SUCCESS OR FAILURE of democratic government depends in large measure upon the quality and ability of the men and women elected to public office. In every city of our country there are scores of men who have the education, training and clear vision required of a good public official, but who by temperament shrink from the responsibility. They are highminded, honorable, but sensitive under criticism. To make a good politician a man must know how to administer a public office; must understand economics and the science of government—and at the same time must appreciate to its full the value of compromise and be ready to make all reasonable adjustments to meet his commitments in order to hold the approval of his constituents. Mr. Marburg had all these essential qualities. He was honored and loved in Baltimore as a first citizen. His friends urged him to enter wholeheartedly into the political arena, where he could fight for the things in which he believed.

We can imagine Mr. Marburg saying, "If I go into public life and become governor or mayor, or hold any other office, then I will be forever like a fish in a glass bowl. What I do, how I do it, what I think, why I do as I do, are all open to inspection by the public. If all goes well, the party gets the credit. If anything goes wrong, the Mayor is to blame." Mr. LaGuardia, as Mayor of New York, made a success because he loved the "game." He knew how to dramatize a situation, and his political antics always had a definite end in view. One of his critics said that "he was always acting out a series of parables. For instance, he discovered one day that a police captain had been late on duty and Mr. LaGuardia presented him with a dollar alarm clock." Through tricks of this sort he helped promote efficient service, and at the same time was able to hold the interest of the general public. Mr. LaGuardia was typical of the successful politician. He enjoyed the opportunity it gave him for self-expression. His talks to children and the acting out of the comics on the radio were all a part of his day's work. One could not easily think of Theodore Marburg imitating Peter Rabbit for the amusement of the young folks among his constituency! In his own family and in his general interest in children, it was the child and the development of the child that he had in mind. He could not have attempted to capture the interest of children in order to promote political ends.

A group of Mr. Marburg's friends came to him in June, 1897, and urged him to enter the political arena and permit himself to be nominated for Mayor. They made a strong appeal to him and he accepted their offer. Thus, he became an active candidate for the office. A statement was made by one hundred prominent citizens of Baltimore, recommending that the Republican Party nominate Mr. Marburg. The petition, which was printed in the papers and received wide publicity, is as follows:

> The Republican party of this city is charged with the responsibility of selecting from among its members a man whose name can be presented to the party convention as a candidate for the high office of Mayor of Baltimore, with a reasonable assurance that it may be acceptable to the party generally.

> While we do not presume to represent our party in this matter, we claim to voice the sentiments of a large number of Republicans identified with the mercantile and other interests of this city who are desirous of having as their candidate for Mayor a man whose name will not only be a guarantee of a successful administration, if elected, but should quell the differences which have unfortunately arisen among aspirants for the office. These differences have caused much bitterness of feeling

which might tend to party defeat, and we hope the gentlemen in question, who, we are confident, hold the success of party above personal ambition, will view the situation as we do.

Your candidacy should not only receive the full party's support, but we believe it will attract a large number of independent voters who have been identified with movements in the past for better political conditions and better methods of government, and who have contributed so largely to our party success.

We know of no man in this community who better meets the exigencies of the situation than yourself. Your business qualifications, coupled with your study of the problems of government: the fact that at this particular period you would be able, if elected, to devote your entire time to the duties of the office, and the fact that you have been a consistent Republican and yet unconnected with any faction, make you most available for that office. We have, therefore, determined to request the use of your name before the people and the convention.

We are not unmindful of the sacrifice of personal comfort you are here called upon to make, but we are sure your desire to serve your party and your city must prompt you to consider most seriously this request. Signed: D. L. Bartlett, Daniel E. Conklin, E. L. Bartlett, Reverdy Johnson, J. D. Mallory, Isaac H. Dixon, Joseph C. Whitney, T. J. Hayward, Joseph M. Cushing, Lilly Rogers & Co., Nicholas P. Bond, J. Hilles, D. Holliday & Co., Wm. C. Robinson & Son, D. T. Buzby & Co., John L. Reed, Sharp and Dohme, Burrough Bros. Mfg. Co. by Horace Burrough, President; James Baily & Son, E. L. Parker & Co., Ira Remsen, George Whitelock, Hugh L. Bond, Jr., Oscar Wolff, Frederick W. Wood, H. B. Gilpin, Herman Wenzing, Martin Meyerdirck, R. Lertz, Eugene Kerr, J. Stuart MacDonald, P. T. George & Co., Thomas C. Basshor &

Co., Nelson Perin, James E. Ingram, W. B. Brooks, Jr., E. J. Penniman, Robert H. Smith, Miles White, Jr., Daniel F. Pope, Frank Kerr, Oliver A. Parker, Isaac Brooks, Jr., Faris C. Pitt, W. G. Atkinson, Alonzo L. Thomsen, John H. Winkelman, John F. Thomsen's Sons, B. Weyforth & Son, Gibbs Preserving Co., Baltimore Chrome Works, J. Tyson, President; Rufus W. Applegarth, Charles Markell, Samuel D. Schmucker, H. Ivah Thomsen, John Hinrichs, John A. Barker, Daniel C. Ammidon, Jacob Gminder, H. A. Barry, D. D. Mallory.

Mr. Marburg, in his opening address as candidate for the Republican mayoralty, said:

You would not have me at this early day begin a detailed discussion of the issues of the coming campaign, but there are some things we cannot realize too soon. Chief among these are the gravity of the present situation, the importance of carrying the coming election for the cause of honest politics and good government in the city and State, and the further fact, that upon the issue of this local contest may hang the determination of an important national question.

The contest here connects itself directly with the cause we had so much at heart last year, and the possible consequences of defeat then were too appalling to all thinking men for us soon to forget them. If we lose this contest it will cost us the election of a sound-money Senator, besides affecting the congressional election next year, so that in this local issue is bound up directly the question of the nation's welfare and the nation's honor.

It was a sense of all that was to be gained by our victory at the polls and of the grave consequences that would follow our defeat that led me to accept the invitation to become a candidate for the office of Mayor. If your choice has fallen upon me, I feel that it is only because I am one of a number of men who stand for what you regard as requisite in your candidate at the present moment, and not because of any individual claims I have upon your good opinion.

I regard this selection as a great honor, but at the same time I cannot help but feel that the success of a man's life should not be measured by the honors that come to him, nor by what he accumulates, but by the forces he awakens and the influences that live after him. This applies not only in the upper walks of life, but in the very humblest as well. The individual who moulds the character of his family or influences the circle of his friends by his industry, his sense of honor or devotion to duty, is an important factor in the community. Everyone should feel this sense of fellowship and realize that no matter what his state in life he is always capable of contributing in this way to the general good. If he has ability or means above the average, they should be regarded by him as not in any way giving him special privileges, but, on the contrary, as laying heavier obligations upon him. Teackle Wallis never amassed wealth nor lived to see the success of the movement to which he devoted so many years of his life; but, can this man's life be called a failure? To the slow but irresistible growth of the forces which he did so much to awaken in our midst was due in large measure our triumph in the last municipal election.

As the guest of an important political club it is not out of way for me to say a word about party. Because I have not been active in party work it does not follow that I undervalue party. Under free government little can be accomplished without parties, and if a party is to make itself felt it must be organized, and thoroughly organized. To organize means not only to give directions to our energies, but to call new energies into being. The use of the party is to make effective our advocacy of principles which we regard as right and true and to place in power men whose conduct will be governed by these principles. The abuse of party is to forget the real object of its existence, and by questionable means and for personal ends to endeavor to perpetuate 'party rule.'

The way to advance the welfare of the Republican Party is to display a purpose to advance the welfare of the community; the party will then take care of itself. A little reflection will show that in order to secure and retain the confidence of the community we must put good men on our tickets. My occupancy of the mayoralty could be of little use to the community unless the proper men are selected to advise and cooperate with me. It is not so much smart men we are looking for—the average American has intelligence enough. What we want are men of character; in other words, men who are travelling to the same destination with us, the destination of good government and Republican success, which I believe to be identical.

What is the meaning of the regular transfer of the national administration from one party to another for the past four terms? Does it imply that the peoples are wedded to a high tariff today and a low tariff tomorrow? Changing with the breath of circumstance? To my mind it has no such meaning, but rather implies a steady and lasting purpose to relegate questions like the tariff to the background, to insist upon purer and better government and to continue to turn out the parties in succession until they get it.

In the city, as in the nation, the tide is in the direction of purer politics, and if we are wise we will keep to the course we have taken and let our aims be to inaugurate an era of pure politics and good government.

In the course of the campaign there was, as usual, a lot of mudslinging, under-cover plots, whispered innuendoes, and forthright open attacks by Mr. Marburg's opponents. Feeling ran so high that he had to take cognizance of it. The following letter was written by him on August 2, 1897 in reply to an editorial in the *Baltimore News:*

To the Editor of The News:

Your editorial of Saturday makes certain charges under which I cannot permit myself to rest.

A number of Republican business men in the city, whose names entitle them to respect, expressed the opinion some time ago that neither of the two candidates then seeking the Republican Mayoralty nomination could carry the election. These views were accepted by the State leaders at Washington, Mr. Gary and Senator Wellington, who then agreed to support a desirable third man. Mr. Gary made several visits to Baltimore in this connection, and expressed himself as much concerned over the situation. He besought certain gentlemen whose names it is not necessary to mention to assist him in securing a new candidate. Several gentlemen were approached who found it inconsistent with their duties to their business partners and with what they owed to themselves to go into politics. At the last moment they came to me. I did not seek the office, but urged another gentleman in the strongest terms to accept it, and would have been much more pleased if some other man could have been found whom the leaders considered capable of carrying the election.

After thinking over the matter fully and realizing the importance of carrying the fall elections for the Republican Party, I arrived at the conclusion that I had no right to refuse to serve the city at this juncture, and consented to the use of my name, with the understanding that I should go into office untrammeled by any promise, and that a good ticket would be chosen so that my administration might represent something.

The gentlemen who urged me to run, having formed the 'Republican Business Men's Association,' publicly invited me to permit the use of my name before the convention. I then agreed to do so. What followed is known to you. Without pretending to a knowledge of correct form in practical politics, it occurs to me that the Republican Senator from our State and chairman of the State Central Committee had a perfect right to insist that someone should be chosen who could carry the election. In this whole matter both he and Mr. Gary were moved by considerations for the party's success and the public welfare, and nothing else. The two candidates in the field were entrenching themselves, and it was necessary for the Business Men's Association and the party organization to move if they hoped to nominate a third man. Having agreed to run, I felt it due to the gentlemen who paid me the compliment to come to me to lend them what aid I could to make the movement a success. With this in view I have been going about to meet the rank and file of the party, and let me say in this connection that this duty, whilst involving some work, has been a source of pleasure to me. The men whom I have met have been of a type of which no community need be ashamed. Many were workingmen, whose hard hands it was a pleasure to grasp, and in the audience, which I often moved amongst afterward, were many tradesmen and professional men. If anything, I felt that I was unworthy of their kind reception of me and of the respectful way in which they listened to the little I had to say.

In my talks, matters have been discussed which appeared to me more or less important. Surely I stand for something in the community in which I was born, if only as a citizen whose intentions and acts have been reasonably honorable heretofore. The people would hardly have me make a profession of faith at every street corner and talk all about what I am going to do when elected. I have made no promises nor has anyone made any promises for me. No one has so much as demanded the promise of office at my hands nor intimated that they expected office. There seems to be a sense of loyalty to the party and a conviction that the party organization must be supported if the party is to make itself felt. It is to this that I attribute their support of me.

You have all this over my signature and may test its accuracy with time.

Now, my dear sir, as far as any personal gratification is concerned it matters to me not one iota whether the nomination comes to me or not, but what does matter is any imputation, however distant or concealed, on my honor.

After the above statement I call upon you respectfully to correct the false impression which to my thinking will be left upon the public mind by the statement in your editorial of Saturday, July 31, that the organization adopted me 'in virtue of a deal,' and ask that as a matter of justice this letter be published in full. Very respectfully, Theodore Marburg.

CLOSING ADDRESS OF THEODORE MARBURG'S CAMPAIGN FOR MAYOR:

You are on the eve of selecting a man whom you hope to make Mayor of Baltimore. Whether your choice fall upon me or another, I sincerely hope it will prove a wise one, and that you will then lay aside all factional spirit and rally round your standard-bearer as one man. The people of this city and State are looking to you—the Republican Party—to lead them out of the wilderness of misgovernment. You have come in for a share of criticism, but at the bottom the people believe in you and you must not disappoint them.

Commonly, men inherit their politics, as they do their religion, but what they also inherit is a deep love of country and pride in a noble city. It is these promptings, higher than any party zeal, which turn men from party when the party becomes degenerate. The reason we have parties is that through their instrumentality we hope so to share public action as to lead to good and grand results, but good and grand results can seldom be arrived at through inferior and unworthy men, or through the operation of false principles. If parties, therefore, tear down the banner of righteousness and justice and set false emblems in its place, if they endeavor to place or to keep in power unworthy men, this higher duty to the city and to the nation bids us trample under foot all lower motives and inclinations, and place ourselves under the banner which stand for men and principles and the common good.

I am a Republican partly because in the past the principles and acts of the party have represented what I believe to be true and right, but principally because they represent it today. With the majority of the people in this city and State, I believe the present means of regeneration to be the Republican Party, but should that party prove false to its principles and fail in its promises, frankness compels me to say that I should not hesitate to tear down and set aside my idol of party until the party recovered its better sense. The majority of men follow and work for their party because they believe in its principles and want them to triumph, but even those who are seeking personal advancement will find that in the long run their hopes are most likely to be realized by a course which will tend to keep the party in power.

This is a family gathering, gentlemen, and I say these things in the conviction that only a devotion to the public good will keep in power the Republican Party here in Maryland and in Baltimore. It is no easy matter for that large body of Democrats who voted with us at the last two elections to set aside their party feeling and let the sense of duty triumph. Place yourselves in the same position, that of turning down the party you have learned from boyhood to follow, and you will realize that we must show a spirit of service to the community if we expect these men to continue with us.

A party's past very properly has its weight with us, but what is of chief concern is its present aim. In national affairs the Republican Party today stands for honest money: it stands for the reform of a defective currency system; it stands for protection to the American laborer, although in carrying out this last principle, a principle on the whole good and sound, the party may have failed to follow what some of us regard as enlightened methods. These are questions the correct determination of which involved the honor and welfare of our people. A Republican victory in Baltimore and in Maryland will help the cause.

In purely local matters we have thus far proved to be a party whose promises can be relied upon, and whose aims have been honest. We placed upon the statute books important laws which we had promised to put there, but our work is only begun.

We must show we have the interest of the city and State at heart, and the people will continue us in power. The step that confronts you now is the selection of a ticket, and the people will judge you by the men you put on that ticket. It is not the social position, nor even the business position, of the men whom you select that will be so much regarded; it will be their character and good name. The man beneath whose swing of the iron hammer the red sparks start in the early winter twilight, to the wonder of the children grouped at the door, will be more acceptable on your ticket if he is a man whose character is good then individuals whose station in life may be higher, but whose record is less pure.

The campaign for the office of Mayor was bitterly contested. Mr. Marburg was accused of inexperience, and incurred the bitter opposition of some members of the inner circles of the Republican Party, although he was recognized as one of Baltimore's most scholarly residents and was prominent in political and artistic circles. The results of the original primary which nominated him for the high office of Mayor was overthrown and a new primary ordered, whereupon Mr. Marburg withdrew from the race. In a letter written to Charles H. Torsch, August 18, 1897, he says:

Dear Sir:

Permit me to thank you for the expression of friendship contained in your valued letter of the 16th inst.

My reply to Mr. Malster on the subject of which your letter treats stated that I had 'entire confidence in the intentions and ability' of the Republican City Committee to regulate the primaries to the satisfaction of the public. No further declaration has appeared to me necessary. My whole attitude in everything I have said and written regarding American politics has been that reforms must come principally through better men and purer methods.

Holding these views, I should sacrifice my self-respect did I accept a nomination to which some other candidate was entitled. The leaders of the Republican organization are fully aware of my position with respect to this matter.

The fact that a majority of the City Committee have refused to let a hostile minority make the rules for the primaries has not affected my confidence in the chairman of the City Committee, from whom I have assurances that everything will be perfectly fair. If I should be called upon to act later on, ignorance of practical politics will never be advanced by me as an excuse for failing to do what is proper, because in so grave a matter I should feel it my duty to inform myself.

The methods pursued by a faction of the party to create a public sentiment against the party organization because it happens to be hostile to their aspirations seem to be unwise in that they display an utter disregard of the party's fair name. It is my belief that in the ranks of the organization are to be found decidedly the better and more reliable element of the active party workers.

This ended Mr. Marburg's venture into the field of local politics. In 1911 a movement was started to draft him as the Republican candidate for governor of Maryland. Mr. Marburg refused to be tempted and the matter was dropped.

In 1920 Mr. Marburg was appointed by President Wilson as a member of the new Shipping Board created by the Merchant Marine Act. The following appeared in the papers on October 30, 1920:

Theodore Marburg, who has been appointed by President Wilson a member of the new Shipping Board, is a Baltimore publicist of note, who has filled several important official positions in the past. Of one of the old German-American families, he was thoroughly educated at Johns Hopkins, Oxford, Paris and Heidelberg. His abilities were recognized by President Taft, who sent him to Belgium as a minister. Mr. Marburg's interest in international affairs, and in judicial settlement of national disputes, is of long standing, and he has for many years been prominent in organizations and conferences that work for peace, arbitration, and non-military settlement of international controversies.

After considering the appointment Mr. Marburg declined. His decision not to accept the place was contained in a letter which he presented personally at the White House after being informed of his appointment. His reasons for declining were at first said to be actuated by the condition of his health, but he denied this and released to the press the following statement:

My position is set forth in a letter which I had the honor to carry to the White House in person on Friday last, the day the dispatches carried the announcement of my appointment. It is for the President to say whether or not the letter is to be given out.

A few days later Theodore Marburg was a member of the delegation that called upon the President and with whom they discussed the League of Nations issue. When they were ushered into the room the delegation saw the President seated in a rolling chair. At first he did not seem to recognize any of the visitors, although he had known a number of them intimately. Then he spoke to Mr. Marburg, whom he called by name, saying: "I received a very unwelcome letter from you last week." The President evidently referred to Mr. Marburg's refusal to serve on the Shipping Board. He spoke so low, however, that members of the delegation could not catch his words. Even Mr. Marburg misunderstood what he said. "I am glad you thought it was a welcome letter," said Mr. Marburg, somewhat nonplussed. "I did not say 'welcome,' I said 'unwelcome,' " responded the President. "It was a call to duty."

CHAPTER SIX

Diplomatic Service

JOHN HAYES HAMMOND

WILLIAM HOWARD TAFT

CHAPTER SIX

Diplomatic Service

An Ambassador to a foreign power is the personal and official representative of the government which appoints him. He and the personnel of the Embassy become a duplicate in miniature of the nation they represent. The majority of the people in any nation know little or nothing about actual conditions in countries other than their own. The official representatives of these foreign nations, if they are popular and well liked, add to their nation's prestige. It is, therefore, very important that an Ambassador should be a man not only of good culture with sound ideas of diplomacy, but should also be gracious and capable of making friends of the people with whom he deals.

Mr. Theodore Marburg had all the qualities for success as a representative of his country. His sympathies were worldwide. His many points of contact with European culture, his familiarity with history, as well as his ability to speak several languages, fitted him for any position to which his Government might appoint him. Mr. Marburg was early attracted to service in the diplomatic corps. There is, however, no evidence in any of his voluminous correspondence that he had actually ever considered the possibility of accepting a diplomatic post outside the borders of the United States. As has been said before, he was a Baltimorean and, as such, found it very difficult to think of transplanting himself in any city outside of Baltimore, or any country outside the United States.

The Baltimore papers, early in 1911, began to speculate on the possibility that President Taft was considering the appointment of Mr. Marburg to some position of first rank in the diplomatic service of the nation. One of these stories was as follows:

A gentleman of finish, culture and polished manner, Mr. Marburg is a deep student of international politics, as well as of economics. His name also appears as translator into English of one of the foremost textbooks of the science of economics. He is one of the most prominent American advocates of international arbitration and a writer of force upon many of the issues of the day. That he would be an admirable representative of his country at Berlin or any other world capital, no one who knows him and his attainments can for a moment doubt.

We trust that this most fitting recognition of his distinguished ability will occur for while it is not probable that he has any intention of seeking such preferment, his inclinations could not well be opposed to the acceptance of an ambassadorship which will enable him to further the peace policy of President Taft, with which he is in complete and enthusiastic accord.

This is only one among a large number of similar statements made in various papers not only in Baltimore and Maryland, but throughout the country.

The sudden death of Mr. Irving B. Dudley, the American Ambassador to Brazil, came as a shock to President Taft and Secretary Knox and other high government officials. His death also served to revive the rumor so widely discussed that Mr. Theodore Marburg might enter the diplomatic service. In fact, within a few days, gossip was wide-spread that Mr. Marburg would be chosen to be Mr. Dudley's successor as American Ambassador to Brazil. The general impression, it was said in Washington at that time, was that if the appointment should go to anyone outside of the diplomatic service itself it would be offered to him. Leading citizens of Baltimore, representative of all party affiliations, expressed their satisfaction and approval of every mention of Mr. Marburg's name in connection with various service appointments.

The Baltimore Sun, in its issue of November 22, 1912, printed the following announcement as a news item:

President Taft today appointed Theodore Marburg, of Baltimore, Minister to Belgium, to succeed Larz Anderson, of Washington and Boston, who has been made Ambassador to Japan.

The announcement was made from the State Department. It came after a conference a few days ago between the President and the Baltimorean, at which time the diplomatic appointment was tendered and accepted.

For more than two years President Taft has wanted to send Mr. Marburg to one of the foreign diplomatic posts. Recognizing the fitness of the Marylander, as a student of international law and as a scholar and linguist, Mr. Taft has felt that his services should be called into use by the Government.

The Baltimorean has, however, demurred until this tender came. The attractiveness of the Belgian capital and the fact that the appointment made today will hold for only a few months persuaded Mr. Marburg to give up his activities at home and go abroad.

Last week Mr. Marburg was called by the President and asked if he would take the Belgian post. The new Minister replied that he would, after all the circumstances of the appointment had been explained. At once the State Department inquired of the Belgian Government if the Baltimorean was persona grata with the Belgian throne. The reply was most complimentary to Mr. Marburg.

This was received yesterday, whereupon the President directed the State Department to announce the appointment.

Mr. Marburg was seriously considered by the President for

the post of Ambassador to France eight months ago, when Myron T. Herrick was named. At that time the Baltimorean was not anxious to go abroad for a long period. Had he been willing to accept the Embassy at Paris there is no doubt that Mr. Taft would have named him at that time.

In the statements issued by the State Department announcing the selection of Mr. Marburg the Government officials point to the fact that he is a member of the American Economic Association, president of the Municipal Art Society of Baltimore, a member of the Political Science Association, a member of the Society on International Law, chairman of the executive committee of the American Peace Congress in 1911, president of the Maryland Peace Society and secretary of the American Society for the Judicial Settlement of International Disputes.

Mr. Marburg is expected to leave Baltimore for Brussels as soon as arrangements can be made. The President, Mrs. Taft and Mrs. Taft's sister, Mrs. Laughlin, will come to Baltimore tonight to be the guests of Mr. Marburg and Mrs. Marburg at the opera.

Mr. Marburg was regarded by his many friends in Baltimore as being extraordinarily well equipped to fill such a post, both because of his extremely broad and widely diversified interests in life, and because of his social and mental equipment. They were delighted that he would have an opportunity to give his ability play in a wider field of activity. Although he had never been actively identified with politics, he had always taken a lively interest in public affairs and had been a prominent figure in any activities that have to do with civic and municipal betterment.

The Baltimore Sun made the following announcement the next day (November 23, 1912):

Theodore Marburg was yesterday appointed Minister to Belgium by President Taft, according to a dispatch from *The Sun's* Washington Bureau.

Mr. Marburg will succeed Larz Anderson, who has been named to be Ambassador to Japan, in turn succeeding Charles Page Bryan, resigned.

As soon as arrangements can be made for his departure Mr. Marburg will leave for his post at Brussels. In the meantime Mr. J. Butler Wright, secretary of the legation, will act as charge d'affaires.

The Belgian Court is one of the most delightful on the Continent. Only Americans of distinguished ability have been sent to it.

The appointment of Mr. Marburg follows several tenders which the President has made to the Marylander. It is said in Washington that he could have had the Ambassadorship to France if he had wished, but Mr. Marburg preferred at that time to remain in America.

The appointment of Mr. Marburg gives Maryland a prominent place in the present diplomatic corps. John W. Garrett, of Baltimore, is now Minister to Argentina; John Ridgely Carter has just quit the post as Minister to the Balkan States; Roland B. Harvey, of Baltimore, is secretary of the Legation to Chile; Alexander R. Magruder Stabler is secretary of the Legation to Sweden; Commander Powers Symington is Naval Attache to the Embassy at London and Jordan Stable, secretary of the Legation in Stockholm.

Mr. Marburg would not discuss the appointment beyond saying that he appreciated the honor bestowed upon him and hoped to be able to fill the trust imposed upon him.

It was rumored last year that Mr. Marburg would become Ambassador to Germany, and later it was said that the President would send him to Brazil in the same capacity. The relations of the President's family with that of the Baltimorean have always been most friendly, especially is this true of Miss Helen Taft and Miss Christine Marburg. Miss Taft has been entertained at the Marburg home on several occasions.

In Maryland politics Mr. Marburg has never been particularly active, but his name has been mentioned frequently in connection with the Republican nomination for Governor of the State and as Mayor of Baltimore. He is generally regarded as an independent Republican and has expressed himself many times in opposition to the program of the regulars in both political parties.

The Baltimore News of November 22, 1912, added to the voices of approval of the appointment of Theodore Marburg:

News of the appointment of Theodore Marburg as Minister of Belgium will be received by this community with much pleasure and gratification.

It goes without saying that Mr. Marburg is fitted for the post. But this recognition of his ability is all the more gratifying because Maryland is a Democratic State, with two Democratic Senators, and there were doubtless hosts of Republicans from Republican States whose aspirations to the office were backed by political considerations. It is pleasing to think that Mr. Marburg received the honor solely by reason of his own merit.

Mr. Marburg's work in Brussels was eminently successful not only from the standpoint of the national interests of the United States, but he and his family became exceedingly popular in this brilliant capital city. The appointment itself was not too important compared with some of the other diplomatic posts in Europe, but he made it more important. He used Brussels as the starting-point for a new study of the whole Central European situation. He became intimate with men and women in the highest circles in the social as well as the political life of the nation. He developed a real love for Belgium and her people, and also for Luxemburg, which has a government of its own and a long and brilliant history filled with adventure and romance. Later on he was to write the story of the court life of one of the most charming rulers of Luxemburg.

Mr. Marburg spoke French and German fluently, made speeches in France and other places, and met with leaders of the people during those years that were so filled with destiny for the future of mankind. He was equally at home in London, Berlin, The Hague, Geneva and Rome. He and Mrs. Marburg kept open house to royalty. Diplomats from other countries were their guests frequently and visiting Americans found there not only a congenial welcome, but left with the impression that the United States was being beautifully and well represented. In short, during this period of less than two years, he made an unique place for himself in the diplomatic service of our country. Although he never followed it up, he was respected and loved by so many people that it would have been easy for him to have accepted further honors in the diplomatic field if he had so chosen.

An indication of the feeling of the people there is expressed in the following cable dispatched to the *New York World* from Brussels:

BRUSSELS, Belgium, March 1, 1913—

United States Minister Theodore Marburg, his wife and their daughter Christine have already become very popular in the Belgian capital and have made the legation the centre of attraction for Americans as well as for high placed people of other countries.

Miss Christine charmingly assisted her parents in receiving Americans on Washington's Birthday.

At a splendid amateur performance of operetta given recently by the Belgian nobility, Miss Christine Marburg attracted especial attention by her dancing and by making the most graceful curtsy of all to the 'Princess' (Countess William de Spoelberch). She had a great success the next night also at a ball in the Nobles' Club. Her charmingly simple and perfect manners have won everyone, so that she is in great request at all the fetes of the smart young set.

One of the high spots in the life of the Ambassador and his family was when Mr. and Mrs. Andrew Carnegie visited Belgium and were received by King Albert and given a dinner at the Palace. At that time Mr. Carnegie was a member of various peace societies in his own country, as well as in England, Scotland and on the Continent. He and Mrs. Carnegie were guests at the American Embassy during their stay in Brussels.

The Christian Science Monitor about this time printed a dispatch from Brussels, stating that Mr. and Mrs. Carnegie, returning from the brilliant festivities given in their honor in Holland on the occasion of the inauguration of the Peace Palace at The Hague, stopped in Brussels as the guests of the American Ambassador, Mr. Theodore Marburg:

Numerous festivities took place in Brussels in honor of the American philanthropist, including a dinner given by King Albert, at which the Cabinet Ministers and the leading notabilities of Belgium were present. Mr. and Mrs. Carnegie in company with the American Minister made a motor tour of the city of Brussels, calling at the royal palace before returning to the legation.

A luncheon was given in honor of Mr. and Mrs. Carnegie at the American legation, at which were present among others, Mr. Davignon, minister of foreign affairs; Mr. Berryer, minister of the interior; the grand marshall of the court, Count de Merode; Baron Van der Elst of the ministry of foreign affairs; Mr. Gavenith, Belgian Minister to the United States; Baron and Baroness Gaffier d'Estroyes and Prince Cassano.

Mr. Carnegie during his stay in Brussels visited the International Museum and the Palace of the Cinquantenaire, and was present at the dinner given by the Union des Associations Internationales. At the recent congress organized by this union in June 170 international organizations and 23 governments were officially represented.

One of the criticisms of the diplomatic service has been that there are too many changes of Ambassadors. The national representatives are named by the President. Mr. Marburg was sent to Belgium by President Taft, but this was done after the election had been held and Woodrow Wilson was to succeed him within the year. It was understood by his friends that Mr. Marburg was willing to accept the appointment because it would not keep him away from Baltimore and America for too long a time. Nevertheless, when President Wilson had accepted his resignation there was more or less of a storm of protest. The following letter from Mr. Douglas H. Gordon, printed in the *Baltimore Sun* on October 17, 1913, was typical of the feeling that was prevalent in the city:

To the Editor of *The Sun*—

Sir: I see with genuine regret in today's *Evening Sun* that the President has finally accepted the resignation of the Hon.

Theodore Marburg as Minister to Belgium and has nominated Brand Whitlock as his successor.

As a Democrat and a warm admirer of the President, I hope Mr. Whitlock will acceptably fill the post, but it will be no easy matter to measure up to the standard set by Mr. Marburg. Appointed as he was in the closing weeks of Mr. Taft's administration, he has in his short term of service represented his country during a period of transition from Republican to Democratic policies, and has filled the delicate position with distinguished success.

To the gentleness and courtesy of the best type of Maryland gentleman he united the culture of the student and man of the world, and shines equally in the diplomatic and in the social functions of his office. I have myself enjoyed this summer the hospitality of his charming household in Brussels, and was greatly pleased to notice the respect and admiration he had already excited among Belgians and American residents alike.

He has upheld with distinction the high record made of recent years by Marylanders in our diplomatic service, and I hope that his talents will find some adequate public employment on his return to this city.

This letter was followed the next day by a leading editorial in *The Sun:*

It is a glaring weakness of our diplomatic service, or of the way in which that service is conducted, that a change of administration should entail the removal from public life of such men as Theodore Marburg.

Mr. Gordon's letter, printed elsewhere on this page today, expresses the universal regret at Mr. Marburg's retirement felt by all those acquainted with the record he has made. There is but one opinion among them and that is that he has filled the Brussels post with unusual ability and distinction and that his departure therefrom will mean a real loss to the service.

President Wilson and Mr. Marburg were good friends in spite of the fact that Mr. Marburg was a life-long Republican. It was partly because of his liking for Mr. Marburg, and possibly because of the criticism of changing Ambassadors after such a short time, that a statement was made by President Wilson which met with instant commendation. The press gave wide approval to the report that President Wilson had agreed to retain for some months Mr. Theodore Marburg as Ambassador to Brussels. This was based on the fact, first, of the personal relationship between Mr. Marburg and ex-President Taft; and secondly, on the grounds that Mr. Marburg had made a real success in Brussels through his work and the influence he had exerted.

There was some criticism and, as *The Star* stated it:

The knowledge that the President has selected Mr. Marburg's successor and that in the course of time he will be superseded despite his qualifications for merely partisan reasons must cause sincere regret to all who believe that the diplomatic service should be considered a branch of the public service utterly divorced from all partisanship.

Most of Mr. Marburg's friends felt the same way and his case was typical of the development of a new attitude between the old and the new political standards. Many people in Baltimore who knew what was happening in Washington and what was certain to develop in relation to the Marburg Ambassadorship referred to it as the "Wilson policies." There was resentment because President Wilson, more than any of his predecessors, realized more fully the desirability of selecting his chief representatives abroad on the basis of personal education and fitness for the service.

There was some expression of the condemnation of President Wilson in the Baltimore press. This was based on the fact that they assumed, and probably correctly too, that Mr. Wilson had allowed the fact that Mr. Marburg was a Republican to make it necessary and expedient to recall him and put another man in his place. One of the papers said apropos of this:

> Domestic partisan politics should not enter into our foreign relationship with men of the caliber of Mr. Marburg. Such a man, if he found himself unable to represent conscientiously a given policy of the Home Government to which he was accredited would resign; but he would not for one moment consider the possibility of going counter to that policy, because he would be acutely conscious of his representative capacity.

When Mr. Marburg gave up his position and came back to Baltimore he was received with every honor by his fellow-citizens. He was praised for the work he had done, and later on he and President Wilson developed a close friendly relationship. As we will relate in one of the following chapters, Mr. Marburg deserted the Republican Party and joined the Democrats because he sided definitely with President Wilson against Mr. Taft and others who opposed the League of Nations and committed themselves to the formation of a new organization.

The experience in Brussels was satisfying, and this period of his life added to his stature and his influence in American affairs.

CHAPTER SEVEN

World Peace

HAMILTON HOLT

CHAPTER SEVEN

World Peace

WITH THE OPENING of the twentieth century everyone assumed that war was a thing of the past. The average citizen of our country before 1914 knew that there were still wars in other lands, but to most Americans all wars were "foreign wars." It was not until 1917, when our own soldiers and sailors were called to defend our flag and our honor on the battlefields of Europe, that we really began to pay serious attention to world affairs.

The peace of the world has been the preoccupation not only of dreamers, poets and romancers but also of practical men and women. One of the pioneers working for peace was Mr. Theodore Marburg. Long before the First World War, in an address at the University of South Carolina, he brought home to his audience the idea that peace must be established by the intelligent and right-thinking people of the world. He told the people of Columbia that they had obligations to the civilized society of all countries and that they could no more escape these obligations than they could escape obligations to their own city and State and Republic. That these obligations were few did not lessen their profound importance and their immediate bearing upon the conduct of every man whose purpose was to do his duty by his fellow men.

In the everyday sense, Mr. Marburg's topic was not "popular" but he succeeded in making it popular with his audience by confirming with rare simplicity and lucidity what had already been accomplished in promoting the settlement of international disputes by arbitration and by the establishment of tribunals of arbitration.

As early as 1910 Mr. Marburg published an essay under the title "The Peace Movement Practical" in which he said:

It has been remarked that two things which profoundly influence the actions of men are the interest attached to what they do and the expense of doing it. Formerly war was the occupation of every gentleman; trade and agriculture was left to the so-called 'lower classes.' Today life has so broadened that war is no longer the all-absorbing occupation. It is still dangerously full of romance, and this appeal to the imagination of men makes the war spirit so hard to curb when once it flames up.

Occasionally a voice outside of Quaker circles such as that of St. Pierre and Rousseau, in France, the great Kant and Leibnitz, in Germany, Jeremy Bentham, in England; and Franklin, in America, was raised against the senseless practice of war; but the Quakers and Mennonites have waited many generations for a popular response to their protests. Not until the nineteenth century did arbitration come to be realized generally as a convenient instrument for settling disputes between nations, and it was only in 1843 that public opinion, or public interest, rose to the point of holding (at London) a world peace convention. The first peace society in America, said to be the first in the world, was founded in New York in 1815 by David Low Dodge, antedating by a year the first English peace society. In America the cause was ably supported by Noah Worcester, by Channing, by Ladd and by the eloquent blacksmith, Elihu Burritt, who devoted his romantic life to it at home and abroad. Burritt is regarded as one of the fathers of the peace movement in England, as well as in America. William Ladd formed the American Peace Society. He shared honors for effective work in this field with the Lake Mohonk Conference, first called together by Albert K. Smiley, in 1895.

For years the men engaged in this propaganda were regarded as idealists. The world looked on, half amused and half pitying the innocence which could foster such hopes. No practical result was expected from their meetings and speeches. Today the cause enlists the sympathies and the active cooperation of the shrewdest statesmen and of a class of men among the public at large who formerly ignored it entirely.

What is true of the general peace movement is true of the cause of disarmament. For quite a long while the practical man held aloof from it. 'How can we demand of any one country that it reduce its armament,' he asked, 'so long as that country remains open to attack by other countries?' That question had to be answered. It was not answered by existing institutions, not even by the Permanent International Court of Arbitration (of The Hague). Seven important cases have been referred to and settled by that court. . . . Two, the Pius fund case and the Newfoundland fisheries case, were of long standing, the latter having for the greater part of a century defeated the efforts of diplomacy.

The court consists of a panel of judges to be drawn upon when it is desired to organize a tribunal of arbitration for some specific purpose. Their members are often nationals of the contesting countries, with all the prejudices pertaining thereto. It is more or less difficult to fix upon arbiters acceptable to both sides. Arbitration is inadequate because frequently its governing principle is a compromise, and a nation which feels itself wholly in the right may be unwilling to run the risk of a compromise of its presumed right. Manifestly that which is needed is an institution such as William Penn dreamed of two centuries ago—an institution which Immanuel Kant a century later so eloquently advocated in his treatise on 'Perpetual Peace.' I refer to an actual court of justice for the nations—a court whose decisions shall be based upon established practices, or in their absence upon the accepted principles of justice, and not upon compromise. It was nothing short of a stroke of genius which led the officials of the American Department of State to move toward the establishment of such a tribunal. The important thing was to take steps to realize it, and this we did at the second Hague Conference. The result is embodied in the draft convention for the creation of a court of arbitral justice. The word 'arbitral' does not belong to the title of the court; it was inserted by way of compromise. That which the convention contemplates is a court of justice. Such a court, of free and easy access, would differ materially from the existing Court of Arbitration at The Hague. It would gradually establish precedents and would help to build up international law even as municipal law is built up.

The advocates of peace point to something most significant— namely, that trial by combat by which a man in former times could establish the justice of his claim only by disabling his opponent, gradually fell into disuse of its own accord and without positive inhibition of the State, when courts of justice were set up.

When the municipal court speaks, it has behind it the sheriff, the constabulary and, as a last resort, the army. . . . We are apt to jump to the conclusion that a similar sanction is needed to enforce the decrees of the international court. . . . We know that social ostracism is, after all, the great force making for law and order and decent conduct, and the contempt of the world may prove equally effective as against a nation which has agreed to go into court and abide by its decision and which shall then attempt to say 'We will not accept this decision, because it is not in our favor.' Examples of such desperate action will be rare—the more so because of the lurking consciousness that it is always possible for the powers to act in concert and meet unreason with physical force.

. . . The moment nations are expected to refer their differences to a court of justice the element of pride drops out as a determining factor for war. . . .

America, above all countries, is in a position to make the proposal for the establishment of an international court of justice. . . . Let the inauguration of such a court, which offers a substitute for war and makes possible a reduction of armaments, be proposed by England, for example, and her enemies at once interpret the act as a sign of weakness and fear. The proposal comes with better grace from America because of her advantageous geographical position. . . .

There is another institution today that is full of promise. I refer to the Interparliamentary Union, made up exclusively of present and former members of the various legislative bodies of the world. It sat in St. Louis during the World's Fair, and at that session, at the instance of Richard Bartholdt, the resolution was passed urging President Roosevelt to call the second Hague Conference. Our own President, it will be remembered, finally waived this great privilege in favor of the Czar of Russia. But without our initiative there is no knowing when a second Hague Conference would have been called. The second Hague Conference again at the instance of America, fixed the date when the third conference shall meet, and this makes much more certain the holding of regular conferences at The Hague in the future. The Interparliamentary Union itself is full of possibilities. A most significant thing—for the last seven years it has met annually. . . . When such developments take place and when the immediate prospect of war is dissipated by a mere institution, as the prospect of war between

England and Russia over the Dogger Bank affair (1904) was dissipated by an institution so simple as the Commission of Inquiry, provided in advance by the first Hague Conference, men see that the ideal and theoretic are no longer merely the ideal and theoretic.

It is precisely to supply one such instrument that America is seeking to set up the international court of justice. Its realization will be one of the greatest events in history since the birth of Christ.

There lurks in such problems a dynamic element which defies calculation. When new institutions are set up, sometimes when new inventions appear, a new spirit is born with them, and that which seemed remote or impossible is presently close at hand. The significant thing is that a new star has appeared above the horizon—the promise, for the first time in history, of an institution which offers a substitute for war, and events may stream toward it with a speed of which we have no conception.

World Peace

At a meeting in Columbia, South Carolina, in the hall of the House of Representatives in the State House on February 22, 1911, Mr. Marburg spoke on "The Settlement of International Disputes by Means Other Than War." His address in part was as follows:

The success of international arbitrations—between 250 and 260 since 1815—and the present frequency of them, combined with the growing consciousness of the economic wastes involved in war and in preparation for war, have projected into the field of practical politics the question of a settlement of international disputes by means other than war. The possibility of avoiding war by entering into treaties of arbitration after the dispute has arisen and after diplomacy has failed to adjust the dispute is no longer relied upon as the sole means of averting a resort to force. Coming into being with the first Hague Conference, 1899, the permanent court of arbitration at The Hague, which sets up a list of judges from which an arbitration tribunal may be drawn, marked a distinct forward step. Its very existence has not only invited the nations to use arbitration as a means of settling disputes, but has promoted the making of so-called general treaties looking forward to the submission of a certain category of future disputes to arbitration. From May 18, 1899, to March 21, 1910, there were negotiated 133 such treaties. The first Hague Conference likewise set the commission of inquiry, which provides machinery for ascertaining the facts, and in one notable instance at least, the Dogger Bank affair (1904), has justified its existence.

Another device for abating strife between nations is neutralization. It has been applied to Switzerland, Belgium and Luxemburg long enough to prove its value. The fact that certain great powers stood ready to forbid any violation of the independence or territorial integrity of these States has certainly acted as an effective deterrent to powerful neighbors who might have had an ambition to commit acts of aggression against them. The world is probably destined to see a great expansion of this principle. Not only with regard to small independent powers, but possibly with regard to certain areas or possessions of some of the great powers. But the principle is not capable of universal application. It must be used with discrimination. The progress of the world may be retarded by the neutralization of countries where backward conditions prevail. It might be well to lay down some such principle, e.g., that neutralization is applicable with advantage only to countries which have fairly just laws administered with some approximation to justice, an underlying qualification which in fact applies with equal force to permanently successful protectorates for the reason that a protectorate in which there is a constant failure of justice must eventually either be left to be disciplined by foreign powers, the personal or property rights of whose citizens are violated, or must be entered and directly administered by the power which has set up the protectorate.

But extention of the principle of neutralization is necessarily slow and subject to serious limitations; arbitration and actual adjudication are capable of much more general application as a means of avoiding international strife. Arbitration itself has its limitations, arising chiefly from the fact that its governing principle is compromise, and it is because of this that we witness the growing movement for the establishment of a true international court of justice. The establishment of such a court, governed by the principle of *res adjudicata,* it is felt, would preserve peace between nations more stoutly than any other single institution thus far existing or suggested. Not only would its operation at once tend to create authoritative national law in the form of judge-made law but its very existence would invite the codification of international law and the formal adoption of such law by the nations, just as the prize court, adopted by the second Hague Conference led to the London Conference (1908-09) which codified the law of prize.

The criticism has been made that the awards of courts of arbitration have been so generally accepted because burning questions have not been submitted to arbitration; that wars which have actually occurred were over differences too serious for peaceable adjustment. There is much force in this criticism, but impartial analyses of past wars by more than one writer show that the criticism is far too sweeping. Moreover, nations

which hesitate to enter a court of arbitration because they regard the interests at stake as too important to subject to the
risks of compromise will be more willing to abide by the decisions of a true court of justice which shall be governed by
established international practice, or, in its absence, will at
least apply the general principles of justice.

A common source of strife and of the extension of empire in
the past has been the demand for protection against violence by
the citizen who has gone out from his home country and settled
abroad. The persistent repetition of such wrongs has often
resulted in the actual extension of foreign dominion over the
lawless country. Now, imagine the international court of justice
to have come into being. Take the hypothetical case of repeated
acts of violence directed against our own citizens residing
abroad, to all protests concerning which acts, and demand for
reparation, a deaf ear is turned. We do not, I take it, want to
extend our dominions. But we do insist that our citizens shall
enjoy the equal protection of the law no matter where they
reside. Diplomacy having exhausted its efforts, the demand for
reparation and for the cessation of such acts would, under the
new regime, be submitted to the international court of justice.
If its findings and its injunctions against a repetition of such
acts were ignored, the lawless country, intsead of being disciplined and possibly occupied by us, would then be policed by
an international force—just as the Morocco, the Bering Sea
and the North Sea are policed today—until such country
showed itself capable of reestablishing law and order.

The extension of foreign dominion over such countries has
been regarded in the past as among the great inevitable forward movements of a race. When analyzed, it will be found
that these and similar cases equally aggravating could be dealt
with successfully by an international court backed up by tem-

porary international police or actual, though temporary, international administration. As to the more progressive nations, except where the intent of a country is conquest, there are but few possible causes of friction between them, which, when examined, will not be found susceptible of adjustment by the world court.

After directing attention to the economic waste of war and of armaments, pointing to the fact that under the present sysem of armed peace the United States is compelled to waste nearly three-quarters of its enormous revenues on the army and navy and on pensions, Mr. Marburg dwelt on the sum of human misery that results from war, on the effect upon the race of killing off the finest physical specimens, the most patriotic and the most enterprising, and leaving the inferior to perpetuate the race. He then said:

But deeper and broader and more far-reaching than either economic waste or temporary human suffering is the question of justice—private justice, public justice and international justice. The homes destroyed, the fortunes shattered, the vast areas of which the economic progress is halted for a generation! The fortunes alone determine whether a given people or its foe suffer the horrors of invasion followed by the payment of a crushing indemnity. Is this justice? Is there any definition of justice which fits such conditions? When you touch justice you are dealing with a great determining principle. Thomas Jefferson termed it 'the fundamental law of society,' one that affects character, and it is character around which all human action revolves. It is the will of man that determines what each man shall be. It is human will, God-inspired, which has made human history. That does not mean that we are to rely entirely on the intellectual process. Instinct and unanalyzed motive as well as reason play a part in shaping man's inclinations. But whether it is this or that set of inclinations which prevail, whether they really become will and translate themselves into acts, depends, as we put it, on the man, i.e., on his character.

More than once in human history has the world been lulled into a false sense of security. We all recall the long peace following the exhaustion of Europe by the Napoleon wars: the world peace congress in London, 1843; Brussels, 1848; Paris, 1849, and Frankfort, 1850, were all well attended and conducted with much enthusiasm. Eight hundred people went over from England alone to the Paris congress. It was presided over by Victor Hugo, and the leading men of France participated. Then came a series of bloody wars beginning with the Crimean war (1850) and including such cataclysms as the American Civil War, the Franco-Prussian, the South African and the Russo-Japanese wars, to mention but a few. By this outburst of war . . . progress in the cause of peace was arrested for two generations and armaments grew apace. The danger is that despite the smiling promise of our day—the establishment of the permanent court of arbitration at The Hague, the commission of inquiry, the prize court, numerous treaties providing for arbitration for future disputes and the assurance of our secretary of state that we will get something greater—a true international court of justice—there is always the danger that another flaming up of the war spirit will again cause the golden fruit that is proffered us to be withdrawn.

I cite these things simply in order to show the urgency of our case, the high importance of every one of us lining up behind this movement, neglecting no opportunity to spread a knowledge of what the movement means in order to arouse the public conscience. The executive branch of the various governments will not move, and possibly cannot, unless public opinion demands it. We must press, in season and out of season, for three things: 1) an international court of justice; 2) the gradual development of the interparliamentary union and The Hague Conference into a true world parliament with an upper and lower house; 3) the extension of arbitration treaties such as our far-seeing President recently advocated, treaties which will provide that all questions which cannot be solved by diplomatic methods shall be referred to an international court, no matter whether such disputes involve 'honor, territory or money.'

The time is ripe. We can secure all these institutions if we will them. If, on the other hand, we are apathetic and inactive we may witness the opportunity to slip by us, the hope of the world deferred till the heart of the world is sick and the nations again are the guilty enactors of many a bloody scene and of wholesale and cruel injustice. And the nation? It is you and I. This is the age of democracy, the rule of the people. The most autocratic ruler today cannot long withstand the expressed will of his people. Therefore, it is you and I that are to blame for the cruelty and injustice that flows from war.

Mr. Marburg, as will be seen in a later chapter, was among the leaders in the establishment of the League to Enforce Peace, out of which grew the League of Nations and after the second World War the United Nations. All his mature life Mr. Marburg gave his best thought and efforts to help establish world peace. He recognized that peace must be global, and consequently he opposed the notion that the United States could stand aloof from the rest of the world. The world had become too small and progress had been too rapid to make it possible for any people anywhere to be secure against any war which might break out at any time. In the development of the modern state from the old tribal form of government, we find a fear of attack from without has become so strong that a very large proportion of the time and attention of the nations is devoted to the question of defense. The stone axe, the spear, the bow and arrow, the cumberous war engines of the Middle Ages used for battering down walls, later the invention of gun-powder, the making of primitive cannons, the utilization of chemistry, the invention of dynamite, nitroglycerine, picric acid and other modern high explosives, poison gas, bombs, highly armored and heavily gunned warships, the airplane, the undersea boats, and now the atom bomb, all of these weapons have developed more through fear than through the desire for aggression. Every nation today protests that what it is doing is to protect itself from outside aggression.

Mr. Marburg knew the history of war and recognized it as the greatest foe to our civilization. He led not only in the discussions of ways and means for security against war, but he worked indefatigably with other groups for that end. As president of the Maryland Peace Society, he was instrumental in bringing together men and women of all shades of thought and degrees of culture, and impressed upon them over and over in his speeches the necessity for working for the establishment of peace. He was convinced that the United States by her geographical position, as well as by her growing power, held the key to the future peace of the world. On one occasion at a dinner in Baltimore in 1912, Mr. Marburg brought together two hundred statesmen and important representatives of other nations. As chairman he said in his welcoming address:

Many of the ideals of today will be realized, and new and higher ideals will take their place. Around what do they center these ideals of today? And around what, we make bold to ask, will the ideals of the future continue to center? Largely social justice? Is it shorter hours for working women and children, and for men too for that matter? Is it better conditions of labor and of life, and of more and greater equality of opportunity?

Is it parks and breathing places for the poor? Is it reform in taxation? Is it suppression of disease? Is it better government? The ideal underlying all these aims is social justice and yet more perfect justice. But let us not forget that there is no more wholesale source of injustice, public and private, than war. Not only is the functioning of law impaired by it so that individual violence and crime and oppression stalk unmasked and unpunished through the suffering land, but in its determinative results there is a finality to individuals, through loss of property or of persons on whom they depend, that operates injustice on a large scale. Added to this is the burden on the whole nation, which results not only from the conduct of war and from war indemnity, but from the relentless annual cost of armaments made necessary by the danger of war under the present senseless system.

Mr. Marburg kept in constant touch with President Taft and in company with Mr. Hamilton Holt of New York and Representative Bartholdt, Mr. Marburg went to the White House in April, 1911, and presented to the President a copy of the general resolutions adopted at the Third Annual Peace Conference held in Baltimore the year before. The visitors urged President Taft to accept the amended treaties that were then before the Senate on the ground that they were an advance over any arbitration pacts then in effect, and were to that extent worthy of further consideration. While Mr. Taft was inclined to believe that some good results might be accomplished if the two treaties became effective— one with Great Britain and the other with France—he was doubtful that these nations would accept them in the form as altered by the Senate.

As we view the world at the beginning of the second half of the present century, it might seem to any person, not alone the cynic, that Mr. Marburg and others of his generation had labored in vain. Two world wars in one generation make the last fifty years the bloodiest period in the history of mankind—and now we are faced with the prospect of another and a greater war! If Theodore Marburg were alive we could easily imagine him saying in effect what he said so many times: "War is a bad habit of long standing. It has been the cause of the destruction of nearly every civilization since the beginning of man's life on earth." He would probably also say that whatever comes out of this new threat to world peace that now engrosses all our thought, energy and ingenuity, we must keep our faith, for the United Nations is still a going concern and is our best hope for the future.

CHAPTER EIGHT

The First World War

LORD BALFOUR

CHAPTER EIGHT

The First World War

WORLD WAR I BEGAN in the Balkans and spread until nearly every nation was involved. The "dragon's teeth" that produced the war had been sown in abundance over many years. The real source of the trouble was the ambitions of Germany and her determination to "fight it out" with her rivals, England and Russia. Mr. James W. Gerard, who served as Ambassador in Germany from 1913 to 1917—coming home only when America entered the war—was impressed by the armed power of Germany and the determination of the Kaiser to gain for his nation "a place in the sun." He asserted that "twelve million men have been called to serve in the army and navy." It was stated by others who knew the inside story that as early as 1914 Germany was ready for war "to the last buckle and strap on the men's uniforms." And others added that in addition "every soldier had a sandwich in his pocket!"

Pan Slavism and Pan Germanism had been in conflict for a number of years. The leaders on both sides were seeking to control Europe and the world. The Dardanelles was the crucial point to be gained. The British commanded the Suez Canal and this gave them an immediate approach to the countries of the East. India with her vast wealth was the principal storehouse of English resources. On the other hand, the Germans and Russians were seeking a road through the Middle East that would make it possible for them to share in this wealth. The Germans in their effort were trying to establish a line of direct communication and highway from "Bremen to Bagdad." Russia, with her influence in the Balkan countries, blocked the way. Both sides believed firmly in the saying credited to Napoleon that the "power holding the

Dardanelles can master the world and its wealth." Others pictured the Dardanelles and the line from the North Sea to the borders of India as a "cross on which humanity was being crucified." Because of her position, her manpower and her will to conquer, Germany held a major place in this struggle for power.

America tried to keep out of the war—as we all know. Washington's farewell speech, with the warning to our nation to keep clear of "European entanglements," was taken seriously. Americans were for the most part not greatly surprised or disturbed when the war began in 1914 but put it down as one more "disturbance" in Europe. Our isolationism was complete. We did not consider the Monroe Doctrine and our intervention in China and our policy in Mexico and other South American countries as *foreign* to our aims and purposes. Our isolationism was practiced in an area outside of our immediate interests. Germany, on the other hand, was certain that the millions of German-speaking Americans would help to keep us neutral. Before the war began Germany made overtures to England for an alliance to break the Monroe Doctrine. It was gossip perhaps, but fairly well publicized, that Germany and Great Britain might attempt to interfere with the internal affairs of Mexico and thus challenge the whole doctrine as established by President Monroe. It was, however, the entry of Great Britain into the war in defense of the guaranteed neutrality of Belgium that turned the tide. America was not a party to this guarantee and still remained aloof from the conflict. The war remained "none of our business." President Wilson was reelected in 1916 on the slogan, "He kept us out of the war." A "war party" grew up in the United States at this time but it was not strong enough to sway public opinion until the Lusitania was torpedoed and scores of Americans lost their lives. When our nation entered the war on April 6, 1917, there was practically no opposition. Our nation went in almost one hundred per cent strong.

Mr. Marburg was one of the few who from the very beginning of the war saw clearly that it meant a world-wide struggle. In an interview upon landing in New York in 1914 after a trip to Europe and on many subsequent occasions he declared that his sympathies were from the first with Great Britain and her allies.

He said:

They are fighting our battle, for Germany is the real enemy and behind her is the militarism which had its origin in Prussia. The war—if won by the enemies of Germany—will lead to the liberation of the German people.

In another statement he speaks of

"the unspeakable trampling of death of devoted little Belgium and of the practice of laying mines in open waters. The Germans, dominated by a heartless military class, are moving back the practices of the world. Their acts are characterized by utter disregard of the international code so laboriously built up and of the common dictates of humanity.

The violation of Belgium's neutrality, involving a breach both of international law and of Prussia's own solemn pledge; the dropping of bombs on Antwerp, the devastation of Louvain and the heartless treatment of non-combatants, substantiated independently by Belgian, Dutch, French and English witnesses, constitute a fearful indictment. Added to this is the ungenerous and unchivalrous wringing of a money indemnity from a people who had cherished no hostile designs against Germany, but whose country was simply defending its neutrality, as it was obligated to do by international law and by the law of self-preservation.

I am not in favor of the United States embroiling itself unnecessarily in European controversies, but a state of affairs exists in Europe, which if the love of decency in international conduct and of fair play and of common justice is in our hearts, must lead us openly to espouse the cause of England and her allies.

True, we are not parties to the guarantee of Belgium's neutrality, though perhaps we ought to have been, and if we had been, that neutrality, with all its possibilities of future influence on a valuable principle, would have more chance of being respected. But there are great human causes which are universal and to bring us to the aid of which no treaties should be needed. Germany is not and has not for years been amenable to reason.

What we have witnessed is as nothing compared with what is to come if Germany wins out. And Americans will not only share the added burdens which will be placed on the shoulders of all nations, but will be open to the dangers of actual attack by men of boundless ambition and inhuman callousness. England is fighting our battle."

When the first neutral ship, the Tisla, was sunk by a mine Mr. Marburg made bold to suggest to President Wilson by cable that this Government might render a useful service to the world by protesting against this new and barbarous practice of laying mines in the open seas. A few weeks later the following letter was written to President Wilson from Lake Mohonk (October 18, 1914):

Dear Mr. President:

Many things have happened since I had the honor of writing to you from Ambleside. They only confirm my belief that the shortest and surest—in fact, the only road to a league of peace is the crushing of German militarism.

I fear that England's failure to realize the unusual character of the present conflict and consequent failure to introduce compulsory service the very day she declared war may prove to have been a historic mistake, entailing a much longer war, a far greater toll of lives and the expenditure of more untold millions of treasure. England knew that Germany had 5,500,000 trained men, and common prudence dictated that she should have started immediately to train an equal number. The country would probably have stood back of the Government despite the opposition of the labor leaders.

In the same way I feel now that we should lay down all the dreadnaughts and submarines our shipbuilding plants can handle and likewise multiply the training of army officers and naval officers and state militia with the idea that the present war will last several years and of being prepared for any eventuality.

May I signify my hearty approval of the resolution recently presented to you urging a protest against the dropping of bombs on noncombatants. I am, with great respect, yours sincerely,

In 1915 Mr. Marburg spent four months in Europe while America was still convinced that the "European War" was not our affair. After his return he gave a number of interviews in which he stated his convictions:

It required no special prescience to foresee the effect the war would have on American interests. The German purpose was revealed the moment Germany entered Belgium. Until we knew what the war portended for us it was the part of prudence to prepare in every way for eventualities. Under existing conditions the act of preparing would not have invited attack any more than failure to prepare has saved us from attack.

There is now and long has been a clear duty before us and that is to organize all our resources with a view to striking the heaviest blow we possibly can strike at an enemy that has repeatedly trampled upon our rights, has outraged universal sentiment, and, despite a terrific contest, is still a menace to the world. We need not determine at this time whether this or that military policy is to be a permanent policy of the Government. There exists a present duty. That is sufficient.

Certainly at this moment we need compulsory universal training and conscription. The President's plan for selective draft is, of course, the intelligent way to apply the latter. Moreover, because of the lethargy that has existed hereto, energy in everything that pertains to the conduct of a war, energy that may be characterized as feverish, is called for at this time.

The President has risen to the full needs of the situation. His leadership is now superb and he has carried with him the whole Administration.

But even now the country is likely to ignore the seriousness of the situation and to dawdle along for another whole year before it is roused to full action.

A four months visit to Europe from which I have just returned has convinced me that, no matter what the issue of the present struggle, we are bound to witness an era of accentuated armaments. It will be brought about as a result of the initial advantages which preparedness gave to Germany and of the shock which the German assault gave to our faith in treaties. It is, above all, idle to hope for an effective agreement to abate armaments; evasion of such an agreement is too easily concealed. Not only the outside world but the people of Germany themselves were ignorant of the existence of the great guns which reduced Liege, Dinant, and Antwerp.

The sole line of attack on armaments which promises any success is a better world organization which will cause armaments to fall away gradually through disuse, just as, in border communities, when law and order triumph, men abandon the practice of going about armed.

I return home with increased hope that a better international organization is possible after the war. There is no opinion in England worth noticing which favors dismembering Germany. What Great Britain and her allies insist upon is a change in the German attitude. This cannot be brought about from outside. It must come from inside through revolution. And there is no hope of revolution until German arms are overthrown and the German people are made to realize that they cannot repeat the trick of 1870. Then only will it be possible for the people of Germany to make a stand against the military classes and the bureaucracy. Then only will they see that they have been following a ruinous policy. If such a change should come about, Germany will be a country that we can live with and work with—one of the most helpful and inspiring countries in the world. In the overthrow of German arms likewise rests the true hope of a wide league of nations organized for justice, which means lessening the chances of war. Any surrender of independence of action, such as is involved in a league which is not merely an alliance of some States against others but 'a union of as many as possible in their common interest,' conflicts with the aims of a country bent upon territorial expansion and aggression. That is why Germany has steadily hampered that work of The Hague conferences. And that is why, unless the military class and bureaucracy are thrown down, Germany will continue to block this movement.

Influential men in England, on the other hand, sympathize with President Wilson's aspiration for 'some sort of joint guarantee on the part of the great nations.' The attitude of Great Britain will have great weight with her allies, and there is therefore a possibility that we may see this great hope realized.

The United States is today the most striking example of the successful working of a league of States. It is fitting that she should take the initiative and move now for a serious study of the problem on the part of powers so that when the envoys meet to frame a treaty of peace at the close of the present war they will come with a plan the fundamentals of which are known to be acceptable to the various chancelleries.

Report of an address delivered in New York (November 5, 1916):

Mr. Theodore Marburg dealt with a constructive scheme of world-statesmanship to be put into effect after the close of the war and proposed that former President Taft, the president of the League to Enforce Peace, should be sent to Europe at once to negotiate some plan of a joint guarantee of peace.

"Immediate action is essential," Mr. Marburg declared, "because of the fear that men will forget the horrors of war as soon as the fighting ends.

The program of the League to Enforce Peace has met with wide acceptance. It is approved in principle here at home by Mr. Taft, who is one of the framers, by President Wilson and by Mr. Charles E. Hughes. An important group of British statesmen, including the Prime Minister and the Secretary of State for Foreign Affairs, had indorsed the principle. The French Premier and the German Chancellor have both declared for it. The Foreign Ministers of other European countries also favored the plan.

The best way to secure this declaration from the Powers is to ask no less a personage than an ex-President of the United States, Mr. Taft, to accept the mission. No one is better fitted to urge this course upon them and cooperate in acquainting the various chancelleries with the project than Mr. Taft, who knows the problem in all its phases and has been such a consistent friend of improved international organization. A league of nations is almost certain to come into being, because the Entente Powers, in their joint note of January 10 to Mr. Wilson, committed themselves formally and officially to the project. But, until it is shown that the league can and will protect its members against sudden assault, until it is shown that the league itself will hold together in times of storm and stress, no country can be expected to place its sole reliance for protection on it. Until then, Great Britain, for example, could not in fairness be asked to impair the strength of her great fleet.

An important line of progress in the history of war has been the tendency to spare the non-combatants and confine the conflict to the armed forces of the belligerents. These helpful rules of war, so painfully bought by experience and laboriously worked out through generations of endeavor, Germany has thrown to the winds. And she has not stopped there. Deeds which men, relying upon the common dictates of humanity, thought it wholly unnecessary specifically to forbid, have been done, not in the heat of battle, but deliberately as part of a conscious policy. Others among the belligerents are not free from blame for giving way to the temptation to retaliate. But in their case we behold the spawn of an uncontrollable rage excited by the deeds of the enemy. To many men the acts committed in this war, the very assault itself, were, before the event, simply unbelievable. The result is a shock to confidence —confidence in the binding force of treaty obligations, confidence in international law and confidence in the upright intentions of the neighbor.

No matter what the issue of the war, we are therefore apt for a time to witness armaments going on at an accelerated pace. But once the German menace is definitely removed by a change of spirit on the part of the German people, the world may not only work back to its normal condition, but an existence of a league of nations—after it shall have established general confidence in its ability to do what it is designed to do—must eventually bring about an actual amelioration of the condition of armed peace existing before the present war. To the security due to her geographical position the United States will then add the security of a guarantee by the family of nations against sudden attack."

Teutons Must Be Beaten to Save Democracy, Says Theodore Marburg — Speaking at Commencement — Grinnell College — Grinnell, Iowa, June 13, 1917 — "Success for Germany in the war means imposition of military and autocratic methods upon the world, according to Theodore Marburg, former Minister to Belgium, who delivered the commencement address at Grinnell College today. He said the spirit of aggression among the Germans springs from their scorn of democracies, and only the 'overthrow of German arms' by defeat or through revolution can prepare a place for that nation in the international peace league which free peoples hope will follow the war. His subject was 'Democracy Put To The Test':

Primarily it was Germany's success in previous wars, and the result that flowed out of it, which brought on the present cataclysm. But while success turned her head it was not the only factor which developed the spirit of aggression on the part of the German people. Back of it is the fact that they still regard the democratic form of government as an experiment.

They assert that while here in the United States, for example, we met the political test in our Civil War we have not yet been put to the social test, which can only come when the land shall be overcrowded and we face numbers of the disinherited with the franchise in their hands. The painful experience of the present war has no doubt modified their views about their own political institutions and leadership; but unquestionably it was the belief that their form of government was superior and as part of their 'Kultur' should be imposed on the rest of the world, which helped bring about the present assault on the peace of Europe. The fight they have put up shows how efficient autocracy is in war.

It remains for the democratic peoples to demonstrate their capability of thinking true in a time of world crisis, of choosing right leaders, and of actually surrendering for the time being their customary privileges and even their constitutional liberties, in order that these leaders may meet the centralized organizations of autocratic powers with an organization which shall be equally effective. Suspension of privilege and liberty on the part of people at a time like this is not apt to compromise their rights permanently. Witness the way in which Lincoln found it necessary to put the Constitution in his pocket at times in order to save the Government which that Constitution had made possible and how little this affected the course of our constitutional history after the crisis had passed.

Unless Germany is beaten, thoroughly beaten, or through a revolution changes the character and spirit of her government, we know what we may look forward to. Is there any doubt that in such event she would succeed in imposing on Austria and her other allies the plan which she herself has practiced — of making every citizen a soldier? The Central European group, combined with Bulgaria and Turkey, would then, indeed, be a menace to the world. Every other nation which had any regard for its own safety would be compelled immediately to resort to a like policy. We should not only be burdened with multiplied national budgets; but, by reason of the fact that militarism leads to war, would be creating a highly explosive condition everywhere. Germany's success is unthinkable. But after war, what? Are we to return to the old alliances, arraying group against group and leading, when war comes, to war that is almost universal? Or are we to act as thinking beings, take the lesson we have learned of successful Government within the State and apply it between States? From time to time for generations great leaders of thought have pointed to the need of international organization. But the ambitions of rulers and the prejudices of peoples have prevented. Today there appears for the first time a chance to realize this great project.

Within the overthrow of German arms this great reform for which the world is longing will become possible. Nay, Germany herself may then become part of such a league. Why not?

When England, opening the greatest chapter in her history, took up arms against the dispoilers of Belgium, her eminent statesman and writer, Lord Moreley, retired from the cabinet. He doubted whether he would be able to stand the labors incident to a war cabinet: but above all he feared lest the war should make autocratic Russia so strong as to become a menace to England. Other Englishmen with greater decision, suggested that Russia's war association with liberal Governments might liberalize Russia herself.

To the astonishment of the world this latter event has come and all the embarrassment caused to the Allies by their association with a Government which had practiced such steady denial of justice, disappeared.

At present the idea of association with Germany in a league of nations is repugnant to the Allies. But why may not a liberal

Germany, changed in spirit, be accepted immediately and with confidence by her sister nations?"

Mr. Marburg refers to the German Kaiser's "blunder" in a number of speeches. This is what he said:

In the whole course of history no man has ever made so great a mistake as the German Kaiser. Milton pictured such a mistake on the part of an angel when he described Satan's revolt in Heaven. But the annals of men will be searched in vain for a parallel.

If there was any nation which already had a place in the sun and which was enjoying the freedom of the seas, it was Germany. Her flag was found in every port. Her foreign and domestic commerce were growing by leaps and bounds. Not only was there no discrimination against Germany in the tariff laws of 'protection' countries, but unusual opportunity for trade was hers in the vast area where the liberal spirit of Great Britain welcomed the foreign trader on an equal footing with its own national. Only the self-governing colonies of Great Britain had set up small preferential tariffs in favor of the mother country. The German language clothed such treasure of literature and knowledge, historic and scientific, that men of other tongues everywhere must needs study it. In the application of science to industry, in the government of cities, in the successful struggle against poverty, in that battle which brings lasting gain — not the battle of man against man but the battle of man against nature — Germany was setting an example to the world. The same may be said of her in respect of at least one department of art — the highest expression of human emotion — music. True and permanent conquest — conquest by the spirit — was hers. She need have only sat still and everything that was worth while would have come to her.

A warped judgment, further weakened by deafness to the moral law, has brought all this down in ruins. Typifying and accentuating the tendencies of a ruthless military class, it has brought untold disaster on the world. Did ever lack of grey matter in one brain and dearth of human feeling in one heart bring such a flood of misery upon men as this? If the world does not actually forbid the continued existence of a system which permits the accident of birth under autocratic rule to decide the happiness or ruin of millions of men, surely it will at least deny to this one individual and to his unhappy heir, who has out-Caesared Caesar, further possibility for evil.

The Great War does not indicate a general breakdown of decency and right motive. It was brought on by one nation, probably the only great nation that still believes in war.

The new movement toward better international organization, initiated by Russia's call for the First Hague Conference, has made marked progress in Great Britain, France and the United States. Germany alone has designedly blocked it.

The need of the hour is to beat Germany. But running side by side with this task is the duty of being ready, when war is over, with an intelligent and practical plan to discourage future war. The latter has high and enduring importance. It must not be overlooked even in the midst of the stern business in which we are now engaged.

At any hour may come that next great event, the throwing down by the German people of their own rulers. All the strife would then be stilled and America would at once be confronted with the question: Are you ready to assume your share in a world organization to prevent a return of this cataclysm?

Mr. Marburg, chairman of the Foreign Relations Committee of the League to Enforce Peace, who was in Richmond as a guest of William Dudley Foulke, foresaw a change of heart in Germany which would win the friendship of her former foes:

I look forward to this war bringing about a change of spirit on the part of the German people which will cause her to be welcomed at the council-table of the nations, and put Germany on a career of more real and higher prosperity than she has ever enjoyed.

If Germany is beaten, and a liberal government is introduced, not necessarily a republic, but like that of England and Italy, there is no reason why Germany should be denied a place at the council-table of nations.

The ideas of Bernhardi, Nietzsche and Treitschke are not mainly responsible for the false ideas of the German people. Rather the true cause is to be found in the cheap and easy victories won by Germany in former wars. The Franco-Prussian war, for instance, gave the Germans such an enormous indemnity fund that they were enabled to place the nation on a gold basis, put her commerce on a sound footing and to become in spirit a young people. If she is shown that she cannot repeat the victories, she will have a change of spirit. It is impossible to stipulate by treaty the overthrow of Prussianism, because we would be dealing with Prussianism and for this reason the reform must come from within, from the overturning of the dynasty by the people. It is like asking a man to agree with his own hanging.

An organization, at least a rudimentary one, to regulate the relations of nations just as those of a state are administered is fully possible. It is a reflection on our intelligence that it has not been done. Germany, however, victorious and outside such an organization would be a constant menace and for this reason she must come in. The admission of Germany to the league would be distasteful to the allies at present, but a change of spirit of the German people would cause that to disappear. If the feeling of distrust of England regarding an alliance with autocratic Russia disappeared with the forming of the Russian Republic, why should not the same thing happen in regard to Germany?

In a letter to *The New York Times* Theodore Marburg, who was spending the summer at Upper Saranac, decried the sentiment of retaliation against Germany in England and France because of the slaughter of non-combatants by air raids and submarines. He urged that Germany be permitted to have the distinction in history of having her acts during the present war written on scrolls of crimson. In his letter, Mr. Marburg said:

No more serious blunder could be made at this moment than for the Allies to lower themselves to the level of Germany in their conduct of the war.

Sympathy tends to translate itself into fact. Sympathy for Belgium on the part of the English people made it possible for England to enter the war at the moment she did enter it; and from that moment to this the sympathy of the outside world has not ceased to translate itself into fact of the highest value. It is probably true that while the cloud was gathering, and for the first few days after it burst, there was much sympathy in the United States for the German cause. This was largely dissipated when the German purpose was disclosed by the violation of Belgium, by the inhumanity which immediately thereafter marked Germany's conduct of the war, and by the publication of the correspondence which fixed the responsibility for bringing on the war. Sympathy for the Allies at once showed itself here by the way in which our children took up arms for them, in the success of the Allies' loan among us, in the moral support which our people gave to them despite the injunction of the administration to be neutral in expression of opinion as well as in act.

England's entry into the war opened the greatest chapter of her history, from the standpoint both of chivalry and statesmanship. When in future men turn the pages of memory and recall that chapter they should find the page clean. What an error, at this late stage of the war, to permit passion to sully it! Are the German woman and child, and, in fact, the noncombatant who has never enjoyed political rights which would enable him to control the acts of a Kaiser or a ruling class bent on bloody deeds—are they to be killed in raids, which, experience has shown, destroy the lives of more noncombatants than soldiers? Does any observant person believe that such destruction of innocent life in Germany would be allowed to modify in one iota the plans of the conscienceless and reckless group who hold the country in their deadening grasp? Retaliation is a game at which two can play, and in the present case we know that one of the two is conscienceless.

MR. MARBURG'S COMMENTS ON *The Power of Right*:

Long before the United States entered the war some of us ventured to express the fact that, while wrong often triumphs locally, wrong universally recognized as such could not triumph; that no doubt it was to deny that reason ordered the universe. Was there ever a more striking instance of this truth than in the persons of two men—the ex-Emperor of Germany and King Albert?

Emperor William scorned the Belgian King as wholly incapable of opposing successfully the will of the mighty German Empire. He bade Albert stand aside or he would force his way through his little Kingdom. This threat he carried out to the accompaniment of blood and lust and cruel oppression. But back of the Kingdom of Belgium was the Kingdom of God; and what is the position of the two men today? Albert reenters his beautiful capital, while Belgium is crowned with undying fame as having done a bigger thing than Thermopylae. The ex-Emperor is a fugitive on the face of the earth. Is there in the whole of history a more convincing example of the power of right?

The entrance of the United States into the war gave the hard-pressed Allies new heart and provided an almost unlimited amount of military supplies, besides large numbers of men, money, ships, food, and other necessities. Undoubtedly the moral effect on the fighting forces, as well as on the governments involved, was of equal value. The war came to an end the next year after we joined forces against Germany and her allies. The first break came in Bulgaria. The conquest of Bulgaria, followed soon by that of Turkey, brought to Germany and her allies the realization that her "cause" was lost. The final battles were fought in the north of France.

When the peace conference assembled in Paris, President Wilson found himself one of the "Big Four" members and with major responsibilities. He addressed a document known as the "Fourteen Points" to the belligerent powers which formed a basis on which the peace treaties were to be written. The proposals for a League of Nations to "win the peace" were worked out in detail. Hopes ran high and it seemed that at last a treaty would be agreed upon with provisions that would make it possible for the nations to work together during a long period of rebuilding and rehabilitation.

One of the first indications of a break between the Allies who fought Germany and the peacemakers was the refusal of the

United States to sign the peace treaty. Subsequently our nation drew up a bilateral treaty and submitted it to the Germans. It was a duplicate of the peace treaty signed by the other powers; the only change was that the American treaty omitted the demand for the payment of reparations by Germany. This demand had been based on the statement that the Germans "accepted sole responsibility for the war." In the American version the responsibility clause was included, but without the reparations clause. The Germans nevertheless felt they had gained a slight victory and it was not long before they began to protest not only to the United States, but to the rest of the world against the harshness of the treaties. They said they had been tricked by President Wilson, and the long battle ensued over the controversy of the question of the major responsibility for the war.

When the League of Nations was set up the world was astonished to find that the United States had lapsed back into a state of isolation and refused to join the organization framed and sponsored by President Wilson. The fight for the League was a long and bitter one. But the League without America, crippled from the beginning, died with the outbreak of World War II. The war had been won but the peace, gained at such a frightful price of men and material, was lost.

Speaking of the peace conference and the constitution of the League of Nations, Mr. Marburg, in a speech before the Chamber of Commerce in Reading, Pennsylvania, at a dinner on April 4, 1919, said:

We cannot but recognize in the Paris constitution the greatest document of political history. The more closely we examine it the more certainly do we find that its greatest conceptions make not only for the discouragement of war, but likewise for positive upbuilding in governmental and social relations generally.

[141]

What is the biggest single feature of it? Surely, the provision for compulsory investigation. That is the item, if taken alone, most calculated to discourage war. The situation provides (article 12) that 'The high contracting parties agree that, should dispute arise between them which cannot be adjusted by the ordinary proccesses of diplomacy, they will in no case resort to war without previously submitting the questions and matters involved either to arbitration or to inquiry by the executive council.' What are the processes? There is, first of all, the judicial process, involving the settlement by a true court of justice of all questions which can be resolved on the basis of law and equity—justifiable questions.

Such a true court of justice is now specially provided by article 14. The advantages of a tribunal of this character are that it will presumably be presided over by judges by profession, who will lean on precedent and, by moving from precedent to precedent, build up international law precisely as the great common law of England was built up.

The permanent court of arbitration set up at The Hague by the first peace conference (1899) has proved of the greatest value to the world. The Paris constitution looks to its continuance in the provision, article 13, that 'for this purpose the court of arbitration to which the case is referred shall be the court agreed on by the parties or stipulated in any convention existing between them.' We know that the awards of the permanent court of arbirtation at The Hague have been invariably accepted.

Peaceful settlement of disputes is likewise accomplished by a third method—*inquiry*. Ordinarily this process does not involve the obligation to respect the recommendations of the tribunal. In fact, inquiry may be had without the tribunal proceeding to a decision. The Paris constitution, however, departs from practice in this respect and contemplates positive recommendations by the tribunal of inquiry. It is provided (article 15) that dangerous disputes not submitted to arbitration shall be referred to the executive council by notice of one party to the dispute. If the council fails to bring about a settlement through continuing the diplomatic process, it shall investigate and report on the matter, 'setting forth, with all necessary facts and explanations, the recommendation which the council thinks just and proper for the settlement of the dispute.'

Now, what is the significant thing underlying the various methods contemplated by the Paris constitution for the peaceful settlement of disputes? It is the provision for compulsory investigation. If any nation of the league disregards this fundamental obligation it is deemed to have committed an act of war against all the other members of the league. That is to say, its sense of obligation is counted to hold the self-respecting nation to its agreement under the constitution, and coercion will be employed forthwith against nations which lack that sense of obligation. This provision for investigation is of the first importance for the discouragement of future war.

The League to Enforce Peace

WOODROW WILSON

CHAPTER NINE

The League to Enforce Peace

IN THE MOVEMENT to form a league to preserve peace, which began in the United States and gained momentum in the early days of 1915, were many men well known in public and political life. Chief among this group were Theodore Marburg and Hamilton Holt. With untiring zeal and indefatigable industry they organized informal conferences of historians, political scientists and men of affairs, and set them to work on the complicated problems of international organization. As a result of these conferences and nearly two years before the United States entered World War I, a dinner meeting was called at the Century Club in New York in the spring of 1915. Here were gathered a small group of leaders who discussed at length the possibility of establishing some kind of international organization that would prevent war in the future. Dr. A. Lawrence Lowell, in regard to the general proposition, said:

> Men are feeling that it is not enough to rely upon the gradual effects of a higher morality and enlarged sympathy and better mutual understanding among the nations, but that when this war comes to an end something must be done at once to prevent such another holocaust of civilization. The sight of peoples who have reached the highest point of development yet known destroying one another, of mankind destroying itself, would be absurd if it were not tragic. Human society has a right to protect itself, by compelling, if need be, a nation or nations to refrain from resorting to arms, and setting the earth afire, before their grievances have been brought before the bar of the world.

With this conviction the League to Enforce Peace was organized in our country, and the plan has met with the approval of the highest officers of state in the leading countries of the world. The program was drawn with a view to the minimum that would obtain the object of restraining war, and no attempt was made to lay down details or provide methods of procedure which must be determined by the representatives of the nations concerned when they meet for conference. The important thing for an unofficial body is to advocate the principle, not to draft a treaty.

The idea of such a league is an old one and has claimed the attention at intervals of statesmen and publicists from the famous plan of the Duc de Sully, Minister of Henry IV of France, to Theodore Roosevelt's speech at Christiania in 1910. It was, however, not until after the outbreak of the World War in 1914 that the idea took hold of the popular imagination. The steady progress of the movement for a league for peace resulted ultimately in the incorporation of the Covenant of the League of Nations in the Treaty of Versailles in 1919. This achievement was the outgrowth of the efforts of a small group of men led by Mr. Marburg, Taft, Lowell, Clark, Holt and others who worked vigilantly during the years before and after the United States became a belligerent.

The League to Enforce Peace was formally organized June 17, 1915, with William Howard Taft as President. Offices were set up and a program of propaganda was begun throughout the nation. Mr. Marburg's diplomatic experiences acquired as Minister to Belgium under Mr. Taft's administration made him eminently fitted for chairmanship of the Committee on Foreign Organization of the new League. He had already had a wide experience with public men in England and in Europe, but a letter from ex-President Taft to the foreign ministers of various countries was the key that opened the doors of the chancellories and enabled Mr. Marburg to bring the attention of foreign governments to the work of the American organization. His intimate acquaintance with Lord Bryce made it possible for him to keep in close touch with the English groups. It is interesting to note that, later, these same groups became part of the "League of Nations Union."

Both Mr. Balfour and President Wilson were deeply interested in the League idea and in the work of the private study groups. Mr. Balfour wrote to Mr. Marburg under date of February 12, 1917, and President Wilson wrote to him on January 25, 1917. Balfour suggested that a "draft convention of the proposed League embodying the best views in different countries be submitted to the governments for their consideration."

Lord Bryce, also in a letter to Mr. Marburg (May 1, 1918), suggested that "five of your best minds and five of our best minds" be brought together to work out alternate plans to be placed at the disposal of the governments at the end of this war. Mr. Marburg forwarded this suggestion to the President and his reply on May 6, 1918, is interesting both for his expression of his respect for Lord Bryce's judgment and for his objections to an appointment of such a body of official experts at that time.

Mr. Marburg, in a foreword to his book "Development of the League of Nations Idea" says that the correspondence was conducted by him to disclose several distinct aims:

(1) To secure a continuous effort to perfect the project from the day of the first meeting (January 25, 1915) of the American group which initiated the movement for an organization of the nations, to the convening of the Paris Conference (1919).

(2) To acquaint foreign governments with our purposes.

The letters given him by Mr. Taft introduced him to the Ministers of Foreign Affairs in fifteen countries, and so enabled him to open up direct communication with them. He knew many of these foreign ministers personally.

(3) To urge upon the Allies the importance of committing themselves to the principle of world organization and to the task of building the world community, before the war ends.

(4) This committee having been secured (January 10, 1917), a further effort must be made to get neutral countries to make the same commitments.

(5) To press for the establishment of official committees to study this question with a view to presenting it at the Peace Conference when it meets.

During the two months that Mr. Marburg spent in England in the early part of 1916, Lord Bryce brought him into touch with his associates, and with others working on the same problem. The American group and these several British groups cooperated closely throughout the remaining period of the War. The first intimation that Mr. Marburg had that he was likely to get what was being asked for, namely, the acceptance by the other nations of the principle of the League of Nations, came to him in a letter from Sir Gilbert Parker, dated September 19, 1916:

I think that your idea of the Allies' dealing in favor of compulsory inquiry and a league to *enforce* it to be set up after the War may be carried out but it has not been definitely settled.

Switzerland was the first to declare for this principle in a letter to Mr. Marburg (December 11, 1916). The acceptance by Spain came to him three days later.

President Wilson wrote to Mr. Marburg on January 25, 1917, saying:

I thank you sincerely for your letter of January 23 and its

enclosures which interest me very much indeed. Your approval of my address to the Senate the other day and your comment upon it gratify me personally and help to clarify some of the more difficult things we face.

Lord Balfour wrote February 12, 1917:

I need hardly assure you that any movement which has for its object the prevention of war in future has my fullest sympathy. You have been good enough to send me a tentative draft convention. I should so much like to be of use to the League as far as any comments of mine can help. I fear however it is not possible at a time when all our energies must be devoted to the actual conduct of war, for me to undertake to offer any criticism on a subject which requires much thought and research. Would it not be the wisest course for the League to get into touch with those in this country who have devoted especial time and thought to these questions, so that when the opportunity arises a draft convention embodying the best views in different countries can be submitted to the governments for consideration? Meantime I shall be deeply grateful if you will keep me informed of what is passing.

Letter from President Wilson to Mr. Marburg (May 5, 1918):

I do not know that there is any special message I can suggest to Lord Bryce. I am always disinclined to differ with his views because I have learned to respect his judgment and to suspect that I may be wrong when I disagree with him, but I cannot escape the conviction that to occupy ourselves now with the development of a working organization for a League of Nations would be a mistake, strong as the arguments are which Lord Bryce urges. The thing could be done privately as he suggests. No international conference of men of the stamp that would be necessary in this great undertaking can be held in a corner or without public knowledge, and we would start a discussion of the very thing which ought not to be discussed, a discussion in the field where jealousy and competitive interest is most likely to block the way.

In a letter to President Wilson, written from England in 1914, Mr. Marburg had asked if Germany could not be urged to abandon the new practice of laying mines in open waters traversed by neutrals. This was after the sinking of the Norwegian liner "Tylsa," off the Dutch coast. Further, he urged that neutrals be notified where mines had been laid.

In the same year, Mr. Marburg made a plea to the President in behalf of Belgium in a letter suggesting that we lend our fleet to England as a protest against the violation of the neutrality of Belgium. He also said:

> And do we not as a great nation upholding the right, owe it to ourselves to strike in the cause of guarding elements of life more sacred than anything material or intellectual?

Further he said:

> As you probably know, I am of German extraction, but national sympathies are transmitted in environment. Would it not make for good and also shorten the war if we were to strike. Any league of peace proposed thereafter would then be regarded as a much more real thing. The shortest and surest road to a league of peace is the crushing of German militarism.

A little later Mr. Marburg instituted a petition to President Wilson urging the United States to protest the dropping of bombs on non-combatants in places outside of the war area. Mr. Marburg was instrumental in forcing Germany to promise not to interfere with foodstuffs sent to Belgium by the United States. He had written to the President and on January 3, 1915, received a letter from Mr. William Phillips of the State Department, saying that Germany had sent, through its ambassador, the promise not to interfere with food for Belgium.

In a letter to President Eliot of Harvard, Mr. Marburg "brought up the subject dealt with in your paper, namely the use of force to support the decisions of the court, and a great diversity of opinion was disclosed. The effect left on my mind was that it is best to differentiate the two questions: the establishment of the court and the use of force. I am in favor of bringing the question of a league and a force to control it to the attention of the public."

In a letter to Lord Bryce (April, 1915), Mr. Marburg said:

The use of force to execute an award is in my opinion desirable only in case the League embraces all or nearly all of the progressive nations. This would include the 8 great powers, the secondary powers of Europe, excluding the Balkan States, and would include the ABC countries of South America. It is only under a League as wide as that that we could be certain of justice being done.

Later on he told Lord Bryce of the vigorous propaganda he was helping to plan for popular support of the League. Included in this plan was that for a referendum of 600 Chambers of Commerce in the United States to ascertain whether they would favor the United States joining a League of Nations, if and when established. He also insisted a campaign had to be made before our people would accept the League.

He insisted firmly and constantly stated his conviction that the nations accepting the obligations under the League would be committed to use force collectively against any nation that refused to arbitrate or to act in a decent manner as a member of the Family of Nations.

A committee in support of the League to Enforce Peace was organized in Baltimore. It became known as the "Maryland Committee to Enforce Peace." Mr. Marburg begged to be excused from acting as chairman on the grounds that he had now so many commitments that he could not undertake any more.

Mr. William H. Short, the Secretary of the League, and Mr. Marburg were in constant correspondence. Mr. Marburg insisted that the national organization should undertake the real task of organizing the United States so as to influence the Senate. He promised his help. He also told Mr. Short that he thought a mistake had been made in inserting in the platform of the Philadelphia Founding meeting the clause "subject to limitations of treaties." He feared that if this clause remained, certain nations might be induced to leave the League or to make treaties that would leave a loophole for them to leave.

Mr. Marburg met Lord Bryce's group in March of 1916. These men expressed a desire to get together with the American group. Mr. Marburg wrote an article for the *Nation* and gave an interview to Mr. Edward Marshall for his chain of American papers on this subject. This article follows:

STEPS TOWARD A SOCIETY OF NATIONS

No security for Europe nor for the world until the German attitude changes! That fact is clear.

But after Prussianism, what? Is Europe to align itself as heretofore in hostile camps? Or are we going to superimpose on preparedness—which, it is taken for granted must now prevail for many years—something else, something better designed to avert war? Recently, as noticed in the *Nation,* President Wilson expressed an earnest desire to see established, as an outcome of the present struggle, 'some sort of joint guarantee of peace on the part of the great nations.' Ex-President Taft is the active head of the 'League to Enforce Peace, American Branch,' the society which is making the most earnest effort to have the United States take the initiative in establishing such a league, and which embraces the foremost men of the land. Its principal declared purpose is to make war, immediate and certain war, upon any nation which goes to war without a previous hearing of the dispute. A Council of Conciliation will deal with disputes arising out of a clash of political policies. Incidentally, a true international court of justice is to be set up to entertain justifiable questions, and there are to be conferences from time to time to formulate and codify international law. But it is manifestly not justiciable questions, nor even the nebulous state of international law, which brings war. War arises principally out of conflicts of policy. To deal with these successfully is the true problem before the world.

The demand for a hearing of the dispute once complied with, nations are then free to go to war as under present conditions. That is to say, the League as such stops short of enforcing the judgment. In fact, it is a question whether the Council of Conciliation will proceed to a judgment at all. Of course, the check upon war would be much more effective if the nations could be persuaded to accept a plan providing not only for compulsory investigation, but for a judgment, and finally for a sanction which would insure the execution of the judgment. But the 'desirable' is not always the 'realizable.'

There still remains in the plan two steps which constitute an advance over existing practice, namely, (a) the obligation of the signatories binding themselves to use the tribunals they may set up; (b) the use of force to compel them to do so if recalcitrant.

Now, why do we base such high hopes on a mere hearing? Because experience, municipal and international, points to its great value in warding off actual strife. In the State of Massachusetts there has long existed a provision for compulsory investigation of labor disputes in the quasi-public services. The power to summon witnesses and lay bare the facts of the dispute, without proceeding to a judgment, has prevented labor war in these services. In Canada we witness the successful working of the Dominion law covering similar disputes, and properly extended to coal-mining, the stoppage of which vitally touches the public interest. In the international field there is the Dogger Bank affair, referred successfully to the International Commission of Inquiry set up by the First Hague Conference. The inquiry showed that Rodjesvenski, however, foolishly, still honestly believed he saw in the innocent English fishing ships Japanese cruisers, and the result of the inquiry was the avoidance of war.

Such a league as is proposed would necessarily have an executive committee, sitting at the capital of some small country, and charged, among other duties, with one certain duty of over-whelming importance, namely, that of declaring war in the name of the league on any nation which went to war without a preliminary hearing of the dispute or an earnest attempt to secure one.

War on land cannot well be made without invading the territory of the enemy. If some such rule as this were set up, the focus of the first battle, a geographical fact, would be easily determined, and there would remain no doubt as to who the offender was. No provocation, whether by threat, either of word or of preparation, nor even an alleged act of injustice, would be accepted as an excuse. There would be no conference of the powers to deliberate as to what action, if any, should be taken, to raise in the breast of the would-be aggressor the hope that dissension among the powers might lead to the customary inaction. The executive committee would be in being, charged with one supreme and certain duty: to make war upon the offender. That duty to declare war in the name of the league is a heavy responsibility, and therefore the fact on which the executive committee is asked to act should be an easily ascertainable fact. Warlike preparation is not an easily ascertainable fact, nor is that of unjust acts. From this duty to make war on an offending member, it follows that the league must at the very start embrace all or nearly all the great powers. Unless it does—i.e., unless it is comprehensive and overwhelmingly preponderant—it will always be possible for the member whom it is intended to penalize to find sufficient support outside the circle of the league to attempt resistance, and so invite universal war.

When the envoys meet to draw up a treaty of peace at the close of the war, men of constructive minds, representing the countries that stand for reason against force, must come to the meeting with a plan. If this had happened at the Congress of Vienna, the history of Europe for the past 100 years would have been very different. Much depends on the attitude of the British statesmen on the question, because in such a matter her allies will probably follow Great Britain's lead.

In England Mr. Marburg found a congenial soul in Sir Horace Plunkett. In a letter to President Wilson, he wrote:

I am greatly impressed with Sir Horace Plunkett whose purpose and penetration I greatly admire.

On March 25, 1916, he wrote to Sir Edward Grey:

Just as Lincoln in the middle of our Civil War won the sympathy of the world for the Northern Cause with his Proclamation of Emancipation, so Great Britain and her allies would greatly advance their cause, already strong, in the neutral world and would stiffen the purpose of their own people and armies by declaring some sort of joint guarantee of peace on the part of the great nations.

In a letter to Cardinal Gibbons (April 25, 1916), he said:

The important feature of the League's program is the purpose to take police action, immediate and certain, against any nation which may go to war without a preliminary hearing of the dispute.

At the request of a group of Congressmen led by the Maryland delegation, Mr. Marburg drew up the following resolution to be submitted to Congress:

The Congress shares the aspiration so earnestly voiced by the President of the United States for some sort of joint guarantee of peace on the part of the great nations after the present war and favors the United States taking the initiative to bring it about.

He submitted this resolution to Mr. Taft for criticism or amendment. Mr. Taft's reply was that he did not think that the time had come for such a proposal unless the leaders in the government had been fully consulted in regard to it.

In a letter to President Eliot on the question of armaments, he said:

The sole line of attack on armaments which promises any success is securing a better world organization which will of itself cause armaments to decrease gradually through disuse. We are compelled to continue to place faith in treaties under penalty of having every untoward incident flame up into war. Until we have secured a better world organization we cannot afford to disarm to any great extent.

Referring again to the resolution to be presented to Congress, he insisted, in a statement to Mr. Taft, that such a resolution would have much more influence and be much more important than a plank in a political platform. Such a resolution, in his opinion, should not specify a definite plan but merely express an aspiration. He believed thoroughly that the next step was to go ahead armed with this resolution of Congress and the pronouncements of President Wilson and get the Allies to commit themselves to this policy immediately. He felt very strongly the need of committing the world to the principle of world organization.

Mr. Marburg was appointed, with ex-President Taft and Dr. Lowell, to lay the matter before President Wilson with a view to securing his support for the proposed resolution. The President objected to the introduction in Congress of any resolution on the subject of the League to Enforce Peace, feeling certain that any objection could stop the resolution and it was unwise at that time to give the opposition an opportunity to express themselves.

He continued his correspondence abroad with Jonkheer Ludon at The Hague, with Count Okuma in Tokyo, and certain others, urging them to obtain a commitment from their nations. He urged Mr. Taft to go abroad to meet with statesmen of the other nations and on August 5, 1916, he wrote to Sir Robert Borden, Premier of Canada, asking him if he would use his influence in Canada to secure a declaration of Parliament supporting the world court. About this same time, he wrote to Mr. Briand asking him to study, in the name of France, the proposals made by the Americans. Roumania, Russia, Sweden, Argentina, Brazil and Chile were all included in the appeal that was handed to Mr. Taft to be presented to them as an introduction for support of the League to Enforce Peace.

On November 2, 1916, in a letter to Lord Bryce, he said:

We cannot be certain that the United States will join the League; we can but point to the attitude of her political leaders and influential citizens. But a favorable attitude would be more certain if the Allies should declare for the principle now and so prove to the people here that the question is within the range of practical politics. And if credit is given to America for originating the movement, the cause would be strengthened further, by placing this new measure of obligation on the American people and especially on the Senate.

The Chileans, the Swedish, the French, the Belgians and the Norwegians, through their ambassadors in Washington, all supported the League.

In an address in New York in the Fifth Avenue Presbyterian Church, Mr. Marburg blamed Germany alone as responsible for precipitating "the present European conflict" and outlined the plans of the League to Enforce Peace to insure world peace in the future.

Passing from England into Scotland a few weeks after the great war began, I was reminded of the bloody battles waged along the border for so many generations, all stilled by the union of the two countries. In Italy for fourteen centuries after the fall of the Roman Empire of the West there was practically no peace. Incessant wars between principalities and between city states made the land an easy prey from time to time for the foreign conqueror until in modern times stable government has slowly gathered around certain centers, the genius of Cavour and the fiery patriotism of Garabaldi finally welding all the states into a united Italy. In France and Germany for generations war was the very business of the gentlemen, followers of feudal lord and petty prince taking only a week-end holiday, called the 'Truce of God,' from their bloody work. The establishment of a central authority in France did away with this anarchy and later on the setting-up of strong principalities and kingdoms in Germany brought about a like result there.

From a consciousness of facts such as these there emerges the conviction that in striving to supplant force by law, anarchy by organization, all the forces of history are with us. Progress in any direction of human endeavor is seldom without interruption. It has its ebb and flow, but to those who read history aright its general tendency is unmistakably upward. The past shows that the group of men—few at first—growing more numerous as time goes on—who have been and are working for the suppression of war have their feet planted on a solid foundation of fact; that the logic of events is with them; that they are moving in the right direction, and that, as 'direction is everything and distance nothing' they will win in the end. For many men the present cataclysm has swept away the foundation of things; their reliance on what may, on the whole, be expected of men and nations, their faith in treaties, in the authority of law and in the larger sway and ultimate triumph of reason in international affairs.

But if looked at calmly the advent of the great war, however extended its area and retrograde its practices, ought not to discourage him who loves justice and believes in its growing power. The war was precipitated by one people, which had bent all its energies to preparing for 'the day' and which alone of all the great nations still believes in war. The backward and inhuman practices likewise inaugurated by this same people are the outcome of a conscious policy of terrorism fastened upon them by their military leaders.

Discouragement is found in the fact that the Allies, embracing so many nations, should have failed to live up to the

[161]

requirement of international law and humanity regardless of what their opponents might do, and, above all, that a great neutral power like the United States should have remained dumb and inactive while the practices of the world, so painfully and slowly and laborously built up through generations of endeavor, were being set back, that it should finally assert itself only when its own interests were affected.

Wars will not cease till justice prevails. The best line of attack is therefore to organize the nations for justice. The first step in this direction is to devise some means of getting the nations into court. The League to Enforce Peace proposed to accomplish this by providing that any signatory which shall make war upon another signatory without first submitting its grievances for a hearing shall be faced with the certainty of swift punishment.

Unless it were a really formidable power against which the league had to proceed, joint military action by the members of the league would not take on the form of war any more than the joint expedition of Great Britain, Russia, Germany, Austria, France, Italy, the United States and Japan against Pekin in the Boxer uprising of 1900 was regarded as making war on China. In action such as this the United States could participate simply on order of the executive.

All of the foregoing had to do with the inspiration of the League to Enforce Peace, the feverish activity in the United States, the labors of Mr. Marburg and his associates to secure approval in the world of this idea, while the War was in progress and we were still a neutral nation. When we came into the War, the picture was changed to a certain extent but in no part did the enthusiasm of the group wane, nor did its leaders grow faint-hearted.

On May 27, 1916, President Wilson made an historic address before a meeting of the League to Enforce Peace in Washington. In this speech, he endorsed the principles of the League and although he failed to use at any one point the word "enforce," his idea of a universal association of nations gave great encouragement to those who had been working for the League.

Without the unqualified endorsement of the heads of State, the League idea could not be realized. With President Wilson on their side the members of the Board felt a new confidence in their work and were encouragd to go further with renewed energy in developing their plans.

A Committee was organized by the League to enforce peace with representatives of education, business, labor and religion under the general title "The Moral Aims of the War." A nation wide campaign was so successful that when the war ended there was almost complete agreement in the United States that some form of world organization for the prevention of war and the establishment of peace should be written into the peace treaties.

At Paris the Peace Conference, through the insistence of President Wilson, incorporated the ideals of the League to enforce peace into the covenant of the League of Nations. President Wilson himself said the covenant of the League of Nations "is so inextricably tied into the peace treaty that it cannot be disentangled without destroying the treaty itself."

CHAPTER TEN

The League of Nations

SIR ERIC DRUMMOND

CHAPTER TEN

The League of Nations

Historians for a hundred years will, in all probability, continue to debate the issues involved in the rise, the decline, and fall of the League of Nations. No matter what their conclusions may be, it is certain that whatever form of world organization develops in the next one hundred years it will be based on the principles enunciated by men like Mr. Marburg and his associates, who were so influential in establishing and fought so vigorously for the success of the League of Nations.

The aims and purposes of the League of Nations, its ambitions for the world, and the things making for strife among the nations which it hoped to suppress, were ably set forth in an address given by Theodore Marburg on April 30, 1919. In this address he emphasized the fact that the League was set up specifically to eradicate, as far as possible, the causes of war and to prevent wars such as the one just ended. He expressed his opinion that the League should eventually include in its membership all the nations who were willing to accept the obligations of its covenant. Of the constitution of the League, he said:

> We cannot but recognize in the Paris Constitution the greatest document of political history. Perhaps not so perfect either in form or phrasing as the Constitution of the United States, but wider in its scope and fraught with greater possibilities of good. The more closely we examine it, the more certainly do we find that its greatest conceptions make not only for the discouragement of war, but likewise for the positive upbuilding of governmental and social relations generally.
>
> What is the biggest single feature of the Covenant? Surely the provision for compulsory investigation before resorting to the use of armed force.

It was this item that Mr. Marburg thought most calculated to discourage war. In his speech he then analyzed the League document in detail, dwelling especially upon the plan or procedure by which the members of the League can be brought to agree upon a form of collective action against anyone who attacks or threatens to attack another member of the League of Nations. In the event of such a threat, the League provided that the whole matter must be submitted to inquiry by the Council or to arbitration, and if no agreement is reached they will "in no case resort to war until three months after the award of the arbitrators or the report of the League Council."

Mr. Marburg was a strong believer in the validity of the judicial process and felt that it could be applied to conditions throughout the world with the same success it had achieved in the local community, in the state, and in the national governments—particularly in the United States. He felt that the provision in the Constitution of the League for the establishment of a true court of justice was one of the greatest safeguards for peace. To this court were to be submitted all justiciable questions that arise between the states. He made a point of very great importance in this statement:

In its usual acceptation the word "court" carries with it the double idea of obligation not only to resort to the tribunal, but to abide by its decision. It was because of this attribute that the Germans objected to the use of the term in connection with an international court. It was at their insistence that the new tribunal, adopted in principle by the second Hague Conference, was called the Court of Arbitral Justice instead of merely the Court of Justice, although the machinery devised was that of a true court of justice.

Such a court of justice was specifically provided for in the Paris Constitution.

Following the establishment of the court it was necessary to codify existing international law. In connection with this codification a number of very interesting international meetings were held, which brought together prominent lawyers from all over the world. The writer remembers being on shipboard with the well known New York lawyer, Mr. George Wickersham, who was on his way to a meeting in Europe, as he said, "to help codify international law." In a whimsical way he added, "The first thing we will have to do is to find some international law that can be codified." In a sense he was correct. In a larger sense, however, the precedents that had been established by international usage, and by the conferences held which had attempted to get at the truth behind a large number of international incidents, had developed certain principles as well as certain forms of procedure that were binding as "laws of the nations." However, until an international court was established there had been no way by which international law could be invoked pertaining to the peaceful settlement of disputes between the nations.

Foremost among those who were instrumental in the establishment of the court was the Honorable Elihu Root. Mr. Marburg and others who had been thinking in terms of international affairs readily assisted in this work.

Most people today, as they look back over the fateful history of the Geneva organization, do not realize that it was really a most significant and influential institution. Some diehards never conceded that the League had any real power or that there was enough hope in it to command the support of the world. Then when the League did achieve a success it was likely to be minimized, and, when it failed, its failure was trumpeted abroad as a sign of weakness on the part of the organization itself. The United States was the first to underline the failures of the League of Nations. We may fairly ask today, did the League fail, or did the people of the world and their governments fail the League?

One of the most convincing statements concerning the achievements of the League of Nations will be found in a pamphlet prepared by Mrs. Ruth Cranston, whose biography of Woodrow Wilson gives a very complete statement of the League and its achievements, as well as of its founder:

Accurately speaking, the League that was planned and adopted at the Paris Peace Conference never came into existence. For this was to be a universal institution, with all the great countries of the world participating. When the United States refused to ratify the agreement made by its President, the League as originally proposed was finished. The project survived because the need of machinery for international cooperation was so intensely felt by so many nations; but the new-born child was badly handicapped from the beginning.

Again it must be remembered that in one sense the League can't fail—any more than a typewriter can be said to fail if a stenographer refuses to write a letter on it. The League is not an independent entity with a will of its own. It is not a world government or a federated union of States. The League is an 'instrument of international cooperation for those countries that desire to use it.' If they choose not to use it that is not the fault of the instrument.

Barring these nice distinctions and proceeding with the history of the League as it actually did come into operation, here is the record of the organization constantly declared to have failed —and to have been a particular failure politically.

In 22 years the League settled 36 political disputes. It administered the Saar territory—a point of friction between France and Germany—for 15 years; and conducted the Saar plebiscite with model skill—order being maintained by an international force contributed to by four countries.

It organized the first great series of meetings and consultations in connection with proposals for the Federation of Europe. This gives only a partial list of its varied political achievements.

Immediately after World War I, the League repatriated half a million prisoners of war. It also arranged for the relief and resettlement of several million refugees—giving them passport-certificates, legal status and transportation as well as financial help for the destitute.

The Refugee Bureau of the League under the direction of the beloved Dr. Fridtjof Nansen became famous for this great humanitarian work. Countless despairing people were rescued, families and individuals given a fresh start in life.

The League Health Organization effectively stamped out typhus, typhoid, smallpox and cholera then raging all over Eastern Europe; and began its worldwide campaign for the conquest of fatal diseases.

The League laid the bases for the reconstruction of European finance and communications after the last war—at its Brussels Conference in 1920 and the Barcelona Conference in 1921. It reconstructed the finances of 7 countries; each case a minor epic in international skill and good sense.

The League Economic Section assisted substantially in re-establishing international trade relations.

A World Center of Economic Information was set up, gathering and interpreting statistics from all countries for the scientific treatment of economic and social problems. From this Center was published a Monthly Bulletin of Statistics, a

Statistical Yearbook and a World Economy Survey—analyzing year by year significant trends and changes in production, consumption, trade, prices and so on.

The Economic Section carried out investigations of immense value to the future on the Nature and Causes of Business Depression Cycles and ways by which they may be controlled; also on problems of Housing, Standards of Living, Taxation Problems, Rural and Agricultural Problems and other urgent questions—and provided governments and the general public with the valuable information which resulted.

One of the most dramatic aspects of the League work has been its efforts to break the international vice ring.

Before the advent of the League there had been some discussion but little action on an international scale to combat the international white-slave traffic—particularly the procuring and shipping of women and children to the Far East.

A Conference called by the Council of the League in 1921 shortly after its founding, drafted a new international agreement whereby the contracting nations agreed to prosecute persons attempting to procure women and girls for immoral purposes, to punish people attempting to use employment agencies illicitly in this respect, to adopt laws for regulating emigration so as to check the traffic.

This agreement was ratified by 48 nations. Another submitted in 1933 at the request of the League Advisory Committee on Traffic in Women and Children provided penalties for traffic in adult women, even with their consent. This has been ratified by 25 countries.

Special clauses were inserted in the first agreement regarding the procuring and exploitation of children—for whose protection in general the League set up a Child Welfare Bureau on a world scale.

The League has drastically checked international drug traffic through international agreement between 63 countries, limiting the manufacture and regulating the distribution of narcotic drugs.

Over 500 international treaties concerning a tremendous variety of human interests operate through the League. The story of the League Health Section is one of the great adventure stories of all time. Following its magnificent postwar work in 1920-23, the League sent groups of doctors to countries backward in hygienic and medical equipment and showed them how to take care of their people. It assisted 12 countries to organize a modern Public Health Service. Through its Far-East Bureau and worldwide intelligence service, deadly epidemics—bubonic plague, cholera, smallpox—for the first time were brought under systematic control. Its campaign against syphilis, cancer, tuberculosis, leprosy, malaria, has been carried out with marvelous efficiency.

The Health Section together with the Economic Section created the universal movement for better nutrition and was responsible for the organizing of National Nutrition Committees in 30 countries. It carried out a worldwide standardization of remedies—sera, gland preparations, vitamins, hormones. It gave extensive medical aid to the Chinese—helping them substantially in their resistance. It sent health experts to every corner of the earth and to every type of people, in this mighty effort for the physical improvement of mankind.

The League Committee on Intellectual Cooperation has promoted a parallel effort on the psychological side. How can there be real international cooperation so long as prejudice, hatred, resentment of old scores is being constantly stirred up—especially in young minds at the most impressionable age?

This section of the League has worked intensively for the revision of school textbooks, for a new and different teaching of history, for travel and exchanges of young people in summer, so that they may visit and get to understand the people of other lands; also for the study of modern methods of propaganda and influencing the public mind, and on the legal side, for the protection of authors' rights and of scientific work and thought around the globe.

At this point it is well to note that the United Nations Economic, Social and Cultural Organization carries on the work of the League Committee on Intellectual Cooperation, and is enlarging the scope of its program and making more effective the work committed to its care.

The World Court—established by the Council of the League during 22 years handed down 60 decisions on disputes between nations. Some of these were on very delicate questions—questions pertaining to foreign loans, frontier boundary lines, public utilities concessions, questions of conflicting claims on territory. Not one of the decisions of the Court was ever challenged. Every one of them was accepted by the countries involved.

The International Labor Organization—established under Article 23 of the League Covenant—put through 67 International Agreements providing better conditions for working people all over the world; reasonable working hours, security against accidents in dangerous trades, minimum rest periods and vacations, care for women before and after childbirth; abolition of forced labor and exploitation of downtrodden people unable to speak for themselves.

No one who lived through that period when the League of Nations was being debated would ever forget the bitterness that it aroused. Men like Marburg, Holt, Giddings, Irving Fisher, and a large number of other strong proponents of the League fought with all their might against the reactionaries in the Senate who were determined to block President Wilson at every point.

The President made a momentous tour across the country to try, in the words of one of the reporters in his entourage, "to sell the League of Nations to America." Everywhere he went, he met great throngs of people. He spoke to crowded audiences and the general feeling was that he had vindicated his position, but those who gauged public opinion were wrong that time, just as they have been wrong on other occasions, notably in the election predictions of 1948! The prophets were sure that Wilson had won his cause but he was followed by another group bitterly opposed to the League, headed by Senator Hiram Johnson of California. This group spoke in the same cities and often in the same halls where the President had received his ovations. The crowds were just as enthusiastic for the opposition as they were for the President and his point of view. Finally, the issue was decided.

President Wilson never recovered his buoyancy after that trip. Physically and mentally, it was a terrible strain. He was a sick man from the time he returned to Washington.

Friends of the League tried to rally the country for a new try. A momentous meeting was held in Washington, attended by representatives of churches, universities, business, labor, women's clubs, industry, commerce. In fact there were about fifty delegates. It was estimated that they and the members of their various organizations numbered about 80,000,000 people.

The group met with Senator Lodge in the Foreign Relations Committee Room of the Senate. Lodge said in effect: Ladies and

Gentlemen, you have come to the wrong person. The Senate has passed a series of reservations and is willing to go into the League on its own terms, but not on the terms the President has laid down. I suggest that you make a call at the White House.

The Committee next met with Senator Hitchcock of Nebraska, one of the chief champions of the League, who was handling the fight for the President. With him was Senator Simmons of South Carolina. Mr. Hitchcock told the Committee the same thing. He said if the President is willing, the members of the Democratic Party would go along with others and we can enter the League on the basis of these reservations. He suggested that the Committee call at the White House.

The group then arranged for three members to visit the White House. The President was ill, but he sent word to them reiterating what he had earlier said, that the Senate must accept the League Covenant without a change of a dot on an i or the crossing of a t. The stalwart supporters of the League found themselves at an impasse. As far as the League was concerned, the battle was over.

Then came the election. Soon after the Republican Convention had been held in Chicago and the Democratic Convention in San Francisco, Mr. Holt and Mr. Marburg, both life-long Republicans, publicly announced that they would vote for the Democratic nominee. They were joined by a large number of their close associates.

At this time Mr. Marburg made a speech to the Massachusetts group of the Pro-League Independents, in which he said:

The convention at San Francisco has given us a superior candidate for the Presidency and a superior platform. It is a cause for gratitude at this trying time.

The Chicago convention (Republican) accepted as its chairman the most powerful enemy of the League of Nations. It then permitted a coterie of Senators to dominate its principal committee, and to frame, and get adopted, resolutions upholding their own disastrous course in the Senate, characterizing it as patriotic. It turned its back on the existing world-organization, worked out by the thought and labors of many men during, and long previous to, the Peace Conference, and by the necessary give-and-take of all the progressive nations. Its vague declaration in favor of the principle of world-organization, while conveying the impression that we were to attempt to undo all that had been done and ourselves to impose a superior plan, was too impractical and too dishonest to command respect.

The time is plainly too big with possibilities of good and evil to permit of indulgence in the luxury of partisanship. If the existing League of Nations is suffered to become effective, the principle of international organization will rest under a cloud for years to come, and closed will be our avenues of escape from the armament waste and the nightmare of war. The way to make the League effective is for our country to join it at the earliest possible day, and the way to get that done is to elect the men who have been and are its friends.

Breaking away from old political ties is not a light nor an easy matter. When the existence of the Union was at stake, my own father, who had been a Democrat up to that time, clapped muskets on the shoulders of two of his sons who were old enough to fight and sent them into the Union army as privates. Since that day we have been Republicans, and I have hitherto been able to take pride in the achievements of the party. But after Chicago I was one of those who felt that it would be a duty to part political company with many valued friends and support the Democratic ticket, unless prevented by a foolish platform or impossible candidates. It was, then, a source of immense satisfaction when San Francisco brought us a platform written by statesmen and candidates of tried ability and character.

Governor Cox's effective administration of the affairs of his own State, and his published views, with their balanced judgments and moderation of statement, inspire confidence in his ability to guide the nation wisely as its chief executive. They reveal understanding of the principles and possibilities of a League of Nations, and of the way to meet any honest doubts of its effect on American constitutional and other problems. His pronouncements on big questions, supplementing his proved ability to translate convictions into accomplished fact, make Governor Cox a strong candidate.

The campaign between Mr. Harding and Mr. Cox was bitterly fought and it was at this time that Mr. Harding promised that he would form a "league" or "association of nations" to take the place of the proposed League of Nations. Thirty-two prominent men, all of whom had been friends of the League and members of the old League to Enforce Peace, signed a statement, agreeing to support a new league to replace the existing one. The discussion during this period and the bitterness evoked brought American politics to the lowest level in the history of our country.

Under the capable leadership of Theodore Marburg, Hamilton Holt, Irving Fisher and a number of other prominent publicists, churchmen, industrialists, educators, and representatives of labor, a new group was formed to fight for the League of Nations and for our entrance into it. As all know to our sorrow the cause was lost.

During this controversy Mr. Marburg wrote many letters to the Senate, to Mr. Taft, and to President Wilson. All of these are found in volume II of Mr. Marburg's book, *The Development of the League of Nations Idea.*

Mr. Marburg wrote at this time to Mr. Elihu Root:

As one who has presided over the Department of State with such clearness of vision and unfailing courtesy, you must be out of sympathy not only with the mistrust and selfishness which characterize the reservations but likewise with the Senate debates which have gone out to the world and in which almost everyone of our Allies has been insulted and abused. The object of this letter is to express the hope that you will do all in your power to help end this situation.

Root's reply was:

I do regret very much the delay in ratifying the Versailles Treaty but it is clear to me that the Treaty will not be ratified unless the President is willing to permit the Democratic Senators to vote for reservations regarding Article 10, nor do I think it should be ratified without an effective reservation regarding that article. Pressure will have to be applied to the White House to bring about the ratification. Regarding the use of such pressure, I feel quite helpless.

Sir Eric Drummond, Secretary General of the League of Nations, wrote to Mr. Marburg in reply to a sharp letter Mr. Marburg had written to Mr. Taft. In it he said:

I was struck in your letter with the statement that Mr. Taft seemed to be a passive rather than active friend of the League, for I remember the time when Mr. Taft was the active leader of the whole pro-League movement in America and defended Article 10 as the highest ideal for which American troops were sent to Europe. You must see that American has not a negative responsibility but a real positive one. By not coming into the League, America has made a good many phases of League activity difficult.

May 6, 1921, Mr. Marburg wrote to Mr. Taft:

I greatly appreciate the tone of your letter, but I feel that my course has been one of consistent support of the League of Nations and of opposition only to the acts and proposals which are calculated to damage it. One cannot read the printed proceedings of the Council of the League without realizing that the League is a going and growing concern of great promise. The concerted struggle against typhus, repatriation of prisoners of war, Government of the Saar Basin and Danzig, registration and publication of treaties, arbitration of Aaland Islands' dispute, rapid maturing of plans relating to communications and transit, attack upon the white slave traffic and of armament questions. All of these are important but the crowning act is the creation of the Court of International Justice. Many of these questions and concerns are ones to which you yourself have made valuable contributions. We have got the Court for the establishment of which you headed the American movement. For the present national administration to talk of giving the world this Court, is as George Eliot expresses it, 'to bottle up the air and make a present of it to those who are already standing out-of-doors.' Is it not presumptuous of our Government to ask 48 nations to lay aside, at our bidding, an organization (the League) which they formed under our leadership, and in fact at the insistence of our President, and accept a new plan of our own devising in place of it? I should have little respect for them if they did.

The great consideration is that support of any movement to set aside the League which you yourself contributed so powerfully to bring into being makes us its enemies. There is no other conclusion. The League to Enforce Peace under your own and Dr. Lowell's leadership, ardently defended the Paris Covenant when its terms were made public. The Covenant was adopted by the whole civilized world except the Central Powers, Mexico and ourselves. How can we retain the respect of our associates in this cause abroad if we now turn around and try to destroy it?

On May 8, 1921, Mr. Taft replied as follows:

Your letter is not convincing. We are working along gradually. We suffered a great defeat through Wilson for he had it in his hands to put us in the League and refused. Now we are struggling along to get somewhere near there. I hope the League of Nations will continue to live. The action of the Supreme Council of the Allied Powers indicates their sense of the importance of having the United States in a world combination to make it useful. We have entered the Supreme Council, the Conference of Ambassadors and the Reparations Committee. We are making progress. For 4 years nothing can be done except by the administration. The administration is likely to get into a row with the 'bitter enders.' The sooner the better for us. Be patient, do not kick over the traces. Be practical and help.

During this period while the controversy was going on, the old League to Enforce Peace still continued its activities. Naturally, there was considerable difference of opinion.

In a letter to William H. Short, Secretary of the League to Enforce Peace, Mr. Marburg made a bitter protest against a resolution that was passed some days before, in which it was stated or implied that the world had not succeeded in securing the organization of a Society of Nations for the preservation of world peace. "If the resolution had stated that a further important aim of our association is to secure the entrance of the United States into the Society of Nations and that the only available means of realizing this last named aim rested with the National Administration, the

[181]

statement would have been correct. But as the statement now reads, it practically denies the aims of the League to Enforce Peace as summarized, namely, to secure the organization of a Society of Nations." The resolution then proceeds to urge support of President Harding whose last pronouncement (April 12, 1921) stated: "In the existing League of Nations, world-governing, with its super-powers, this Republic will have no part." Mr. Marburg said:

This is equivocal and urging support of Secretary Hughes in working out a plan which will accomplish these purposes is ridiculous. In other words, the League to Enforce Peace is now to come out flatly in support of a policy to scrap the League. Mr. Taft and many others of us have said repeatedly in print that the Paris Covenant does not set up a super-government. We have said in effect that it was a great and beneficent document and that its adoption would open a new era for mankind. Now that the Covenant has been adopted are we to eat our words and be disloyal to the cause as well as to our martyred ex-President and traitors to the principles for which we have given so much time, finance and personal attention during these fateful years?

Quoting Mr. Harding's frequent expressions in favor of "an association of nations" to discourage wars, Mr. Marburg said:

It is more and more evident that *this* League of Nations— not *some* League of Nations—is the hope of the world. The administration think they have a mandate to keep out of the League. Surely they do not go so far as to interpret the Presidential vote as a command to kill the League?

In this period of uncertainty, when the country was so divided between pro-League and anti-League, a number of thoughtful men began to seek some way out of the impasse. Among the proposals was the suggestion that even if we could not agree upon the League, at least we could agree upon the Court. Membership in the World Court thus became a real issue. The matter was discussed at length not only in the United States but throughout the world. In one of the meetings held in Geneva at that time, Mr. Briand, Sir John Simons, and other leaders from the member nations of the League met to discuss the matter. The question was asked if they would be willing to put the International Court in first place in their thinking, or at least give it the authority that would make it a strong and new safeguard against war. Briand in a jovial mood said, "We will accept the Court but we French do not like a *Court*. Court means prison, punishment and that somebody has not been behaving. We believe in the Court as a safeguard of our liberty and as a prevention of crime, and to be used for the administration of law and to intimidate as well as to punish criminals. However, we have an innate dislike of the idea of being run by a Court. We try to stay away from court. But if you Americans, who I am told are ruled by your Supreme Court, think it would bring you into the Society of Nations and help to prevent war, we will go along with you in the mattter."

This was only one of the suggestions that were made designed to by-pass the League and to get something in its place. In all these controversies Mr. Marburg showed his breadth of interest and the keenness of his intellect. Of the Court he said:

The new Court of International Justice, before which conflicts of rights may be determined, adds another institution of great value and our plea is that America, which officially and through private endeavor labored so long for it, may be allowed to adhere to it. The origin of most of our sound institutions is in the needs of the community. There is very great need for this Court which will help to crystallize and give authority to the more commonly accepted practices in international relations.

The Briand-Kellogg Pact Outlawing War began with a fanfare and a promise that was never realized. The authorities of this new plan were among the most bitter opponents of the League. The arguments ran something like this: "if you outlaw war, then you are killing it. We have put it on the black-list and will have nothing further to do with it." It had a certain appeal, particularly in groups within the churches. Professor James Shotwell, although he had very little confidence in the plan to "outlaw war," suggested it, first of all, to Mr. Briand in Paris. Mr. Briand came to the United States and laid it before President Coolidge. Coolidge was favorable to the idea. It was suggested that instead of making a pact between France and the United States the compact be open to the world. The Briand-Kellogg Pact was drawn up and was signed by practically all the nations. Among many of the hysterical speeches of the time was one particularly outstanding, in that it expressed the extreme enthusiasm and hysteria over the treaty outlawing war. This gentleman said to a group of churchmen: "Now that war is a thing of the past, you ministers may turn your attention to the proper work of the church and not spend so much time on international affairs." The Briand-Kellogg Pact was an empty gesture. There was no bite to it and had no authority to effect a compromise—let alone to prevent war or lessen its danger.

Mr. Marburg pointed out in a letter to *The New York Times* that "the Pact of Paris meets with a real difficulty in that it has no provision for its application." The United States was a prime mover of the Pact, and Secretary Stimson promised that we would consult with the other signatories in the event there was a threatened violation. Mr. Marburg asked the question: "Did not Italy give the world ample notice of what she was planning to do to Ethiopia and did we so much as lift our little finger, which it was our duty as originators of the Pact to do?" He continued, "The world has ample power both under the League Covenant and the Briand-Kellogg Pact to stop aggression. Our need today is for fearless application of existing treaties."

The League of Nations did not fail. The nations and their peoples failed the League. The fight goes on and now that we have gone through another war and are still—five years after it has ended—living in a world technically, if not actually at war, it is futile, but only human, to speculate on what might have happened if the United States had wholeheartedly supported the League which it had brought into existence.

Mr. Marburg never lost his conviction or his optimism. "The World," he said, "may never enjoy international union as complete as that of the states of the American Union. But every approach to it, provided it is based on the solemn pledge to put down war between the states, will strengthen the general sense of security and lessen the need for strategic boundaries and armaments. The League is dead—long live the League."

ARISTIDE BRIAND

War Again

CHAPTER ELEVEN

War Again

THROUGHOUT THE LONG recorded history of mankind, stretching over six thousand years, there have been just over six thousand major wars besides innumerable "border incidents." Almost every one of these wars grew out of the preceding war. The Greeks in their mythology picture war as a giant sowing dragons' teeth, which in time sprang up into rows and battalions of armed soldiers. The reason that war has persisted is because even from the earliest days it has been much easier to arouse people and nations to war than to secure their cooperation in establishing peace. As the centuries have passed, the difficulties of making peace have become more complex, while at the same time the facilities for making war have increased.

In the opening years of the 20th Century Mr. Theodore Marburg associated himself closely with that important group of men who were thinking and planning for peace.

Alfred Bernhard Nobel, who died in 1896, bequeathed his entire fortune to the "Nobel Prize Foundation." The first prize for peace was given in 1901.

Andrew Carnegie and many other optimists were full of hopes for a world from which the fear and danger of war would be removed. In spite of serious differences and rebuffs, The Hague Conferences, beginning with the first one in 1899, seemed to give promise of this better future. Agreement was reached upon plans for an International Court of Arbitration. The Carnegie Endowment for International Peace was formally endowed and began operation in 1910. The Carnegie Peace Palace was dedicated at The Hague in 1913. Many peace societies sprang into existence during this period. In February, 1914, Mr. Carnegie established and endowed the Church Peace Union. Theodore Marburg took an active interest in the effort to enlist the churches in these worldwide plans. The Church Peace Union started its work with the strong conviction that "military power alone cannot maintain peace." Religion, reason, humane considerations, as well as self-interest, led the movement for finishing the unfinished task of "saving succeeding generations from the scourge of war."

In face of what has happened during these last forty years it is hard to reconcile the dreams of these earlier years with the hard facts in the international situation today. People in all lands were badly informed of conditions, and those who did know the truth refused to see that with the changes in economic and social life throughout the West the methods and means for making war had also completely changed. People in all countries lived with blinders on their eyes; while at the same time the growth of international trade and its rivalries were presenting new issues. President Ralph Hutchinson of Lafayette College said in a speech made in New York City recently that "in the last fifty years since the beginning of this century more wars have been fought, more men killed and wounded in battle, more cities devastated, more civilians murdered, than in all the 800 years preceding January 1, 1950."

At the first meeting of the Church Peace Union Mr. Carnegie said:

We meet today under wholly exceptional conditions, for never in the history of man has such a body assembled for such a purpose; no less than twelve of the chief religious bodies of the civilized world being here represented by their prominent official leaders . . . to cooperate as one body in the holy task of abolishing war. . . . Certain that the strongest appeal can be made to religious bodies, I hereby appeal, hoping that you will feel it to be not only your duty but your pleasure to undertake the administration of a fund, the income of which will be used as in your judgment will most successfully appeal to the people in the cause of peace through arbitration of international disputes.

The first message issued by the Church Peace Union was released the same day that Mr. Carnegie called the group together. The message dealt with four problems: international trends, war expenditures, taxes, and trade. These are the issues that are foremost in our thinking today, although they may be stated in somewhat different form. We are still seeking a way to meet the demands brought about by the modern and fast-moving social transitions of our time. There is a new awareness of our responsibility to our fellowmen throughout the world. The challenging social changes have been brought about by the teachings of our Western educational systems, our religious contacts, and the impact made upon other political and cultural systems by the implications of democracy. How can we meet these demands? How can we stop the huge expenditures that are consuming the major part of all the current resources of the nations and their people, and mortgaging their future for an indeterminable period of time? In this statement the Trustees also expressed their alarm over the fact that "the combined debt of the world, mostly borrowed and used for war purposes, amounts to nearly 37 billion dollars." This sounds like small change when placed beside the combined debt of the world today. The gross debt of the United States in 1914 was approximately $1,150,000,000—or about $12. per person. In 1948 the debt in the United States alone had increased to $252,292,246,513, or approximately $1,700 for every man, woman and child in the United States! The total cost to all the nations of World War II is estimated at the astronomical figure of more than 1,000 Billion Dollars.

The Second World War was made inevitable when the United States refused to join the League of Nations. After having refused to join, we began to treat the organization as though what it did were of no concern to us whatsoever. Our Secretary of State, for a period, even refused to acknowledge letters sent to Washington by the officers of the League. Many individuals in the United States, who had worked long and eagerly for international peace, were aghast. Men like Mr. Marburg, Mr. Shotwell, Mr. Holt, and many, many others tried in every possible way to secure enough cooperation so that we could undo some of the damage created by the attitude of our Government. A long list of such efforts attest to the fidelity of these men to their ideals.

Fascism in Italy was older than Mussolini. A long struggle had been carried on over a great number of years. Count Sforza, as well as many others who were intimately acquainted with Italy, recounts how Mussolini took advantage of the disillusionment and strife among the parties themselves. The noble families were divided, one against the other, and had been for centuries. The labor groups attained power—and with the infiltration of communist principles they undertook to capture the government itself. In fact, in some of the northern factories, particularly in the automobile industry, they were able to gain control of a considerable amount of the economic life of the cities. Trouble developed when they attempted to get new material to carry on the work, and the contracting parties outside of those cities refused to make deliveries. The banks held up credit and froze the accounts of the companies, so that they could not pay wages or carry on business in the usual manner. The railroads refused to deliver to the companies or to carry their products. Thus the whole economic system flattened out and the country was ripe for revolution. The "March on Rome" was a part of this process. Mussolini and his advisers saw their opportunity and took things into their own hands.

Count Sforza had a deep sympathy for Mussolini. He felt that he was so weak "that," as he said, "I have authentic pity for him." He also reported that he had often warned Raymond Poincaire, Austen Chamberlin and other leaders of the outside nations not to take Mussolini too seriously, for he feared foreign statesmen with their want of imagination and lack of courage would be the veritable authors of a war they were all fearing. During those years no one in France, in England, or in the United States wanted to see clearly. Sforza said:

And to think, that poor Mussolini at the very summit of his power sent to me, as his envoy, one of my colleagues in the Italian Senate, a member of the Sicilian aristocracy, to offer me the assurance that my estates would not be confiscated if only while continuing to condemn Fascism, I would from time to time remark in my books and articles: but it cannot be denied that Mussolini has genius. I had my final talk with Mussolini, then dictator in Rome. I had been declining one after another all his offers when he rose and said: but don't you know that I can have you placed against a wall and shot? It was ironical but pleasing to see how the menacing Mussolini was taken aback by my rejoinder as I smiled and said, And afterwards?

Mussolini greatly influenced Adolf Hitler. Conditions in Germany were not good. The people were dissatisfied and they felt they had been robbed of victory in World War I—not in the field of battle but by allied diplomacy. Everywhere one heard the cry, "We Germans refuse to remain second-class citizens of the world." When he came into power Hitler's brutality at once aroused and alarmed the rest of the world. We who lived through the period prior to the outbreak of World War II will never forget these facts: the mistaken efforts to appease a mad man; permission to rearm the Germans and Hitler's march into the Rhineland; the acquiescence in the betrayal of Czechoslovakia. The late-lamented

Jan Masaryk said bitterly of the Munich Conference that a major operation was about to be performed; that his country was the invalid and victim that was to be operated on by the trained doctors in diplomacy of the Great Powers; that they, the doctors, were allowed in the operating chamber with their nurses and advisers but the victim, the patient on whom the operation was to be performed, was not permitted to be present!

Many Germans did not like Hitler but they were hopelessly in the minority. When the attack came on Poland war on a world-wide scale became inevitable.

Mr. Marburg, in the speeches he made and the letters he wrote, put the blame squarely where it belongs: on Hitler. An amusing story was told about the meeting between Hitler and Mussolini in Venice. Mussolini and his entourage had everything in order and were waiting in the old Royal Palace. Hitler and his group entered. Very stiff and pompous, Hitler advanced and gave the Nazi salute bending low and saying, "Heil Imperator." Whereupon Mussolini gave the Fascist salute and bending equally low replied, "Heil Imitatur."

Sturzo, writing of the Second World War, quotes President Roosevelt saying "Mussolini stabbed France in the back." This, he says, is not accurate, for fascism began its anti-French policy in 1927 by demanding Nice, Savoy, Corsica and Tunis. This propaganda was intensified after Munich. Sturzo then goes on to remark that "there is no one so deaf who will not hear," and then buttresses this statement with the fact that everyone should have known what Mussolini had in mind. He dared to oppose the League of Nations. He arranged for the invasion of Ethiopia. Many of us were present and saw Mussolini's reporters at Geneva thumb their noses at Emperor Haille Salassie. He also points out that Hitler had written in full in *Mein Kampf*, the story of his life and his battle, everything that he proposed to do to the last "belt, bolt and buckle" and nobody took it seriously.

Mr. Marburg wrote extensively and spoke on many occasions regarding the serious situation that faced the world. He was something of a prophet in that he pointed out the results that would follow another war. In a letter written to *The New York Times* in the early part of 1938 he said:

> In 1914, through lack of world councils, we had nothing to say as to whether or not there should be war. We leaned backward—did we not?—in a vain attempt to keep out of it. In other words we were not free men: we were slaves of circumstance.
>
> But men can be masters of circumstance. How? By foresight and organization! In world affairs this means assuming responsibilities. We should assure today the remaining members of the League of Nations that the Briand-Kellogg Pact means something to us and that we will unite with them in punishing the aggressor in Europe and in the Western world generally, and will lend our navy and army and economic resources to that end. If we do this there will be no war in Europe.
>
> Couple with this offer two conditions: the transfer of all mandated territories to the League of Nations to be administered by it, and a promise by the leading industrial countries of Europe that they will approximate the hours and wages of labor current in the United States.
>
> Germany's appetite grows with what it feeds on. Her absorption of the German-speaking people of Austria would have been allowed by Europe long ago if it had trusted her. To accede now to her demand for the return of her lost colonies would not help the cause of peace.

On November 4, 1918, I cabled Lord Bryce: 'Why not international administration for German colonies in Africa and Asia Minor? Excellent impression if England voluntarily proclaimed such policy.' In his reply, November 21, 1918, he said: 'I agree in principle. * * * We, in England, really don't want any new territory for ourselves, but it is hard to resist the demands of our colonies who have been endangered by enemy intrigues.' It will be recalled that it was similarly the colonies who blocked the demand for the abolition of slavery in the British Empire, a cause for which Wilberforce had to fight for thirty years in Parliament before it triumphed.

In 1918 the London Interallied Labor and Socialist Conference demanded that certain regions, then dominated by the Turks, be administered directly by the League of Nations. That recommendation was accepted by other groups and extended to all undeveloped regions and backward peoples incapable of self-government.

Under League administration all countries would, of course, receive like treatment in matter both of trade and concessions. Such a regime, applied to the former German colonies in common with other regions at present mandated, should satisfy all legitimate aspirations of the 'have-not' countries.

And actual ownership of vast territories would help to establish the League of Nations as a lasting institution, just as the action of certain of the American States in ceding to the Federal Government all their Western lands, out of which the States of the Middle West were later carved, helped to make the United States a going concern. It should not be difficult to win over to this program Germany's ally, Italy, unless she has an understanding with Germany by which she will be backed up in an attempt to appropriate Yugoslavia as reward for countenancing Germany's Austrian adventure.

As to the second condition, which should be coupled with our promise to help safeguard the peace, our liberal policy with respect to the hours and wages of labor cannot succeed unless other industrial countries approximate both.

The success of such a foreign policy as above outlined would bring lasting gains of immeasurable value: more enduring peace, economic revival resulting from a sense of political security, and ever lower hours and higher wages for labor as future industrial progress justified it.

In another letter written at about the same time, Mr. Marburg said:

The world leadership the United States had under Woodrow Wilson is completely gone. It was leadership for the good of all and therefore for our own good which is tied up with the good of all. Because of our attitude toward the Japanese, England gave up her alliance with Japan. At the invitation of our Government she took part in the Washington Naval Conference of 1922, scuttled part of her fleet and abstained from building as a result of the conference. She then based her policy and placed her reliance on the collective security supposed to reside in the League of Nations with the founding of which Woodrow Wilson, to his credit, had more to do than any other single individual and which was fatally weakened by our failure to join it. Japan is now an ally of England's potential enemies, Germany and Italy; and the English fleet is still too weak for England's needs. Are we displaying now a manly and proper sense of responsibility for that situation?

In September, 1938, a group of six prominent Baltimoreans sent a telegram to President Roosevelt, suggesting that the Government invite representatives from the four principal powers of Europe, excluding Russia, for a meeting in Washington to discuss a settlement of the Czechoslovakian issue. Signed by Dr. Isaiah Bowman, president of Johns Hopkins University; Dr. David Allan Robertson, president of Goucher College; the Rt. Rev. Edward E. Helfenstein, Protestant Episcopal Bishop of Maryland; Dr. John M. T. Finney; the Rev. Dr. Harold N. Arrowsmith, and Mr. Theodore Marburg, the message was as follows:

Supplementing your important message appealing for a peace treaty before instead of after hostilities, why not have the United States suggest to Germany, England, France and Italy a suspension of the Czechoslovakia issue until these four powers shall have met in an attempt to thrash out all the causes for dissension among them. The conferees to meet in Washington as guests of the United States. This suggestion does not involve any concession on the part of any of them except the withdrawal of Hitler's time limit.

(NOTE: This message was given to Western Union for despatch at 8:30 to 9 P.M. September 26th. According to statement in *Baltimore Sun* of September 29th, the President's message to Hitler was sent early in the evening of September 27th—appealing for a conference of the Powers. The President's message was drawn up with Secretary Hull and Mr. Welles present.)

On the night of September 27, 1938, President Roosevelt cabled to the Chancellor of Germany, as follows:

I desire to acknowledge Your Excellency's reply to my telegram of September 26. I was confident that you would coincide in the opinion I expressed regarding the unforeseeable consequences and the incalculable disaster which would result to the entire world from the outbreak of a European war.

The question before the world today, Mr. Chancellor, is not the question of errors of judgment or of injustices committed in the past. It is the question of the fate of the world today and tomorrow. The world asks of us who are at this moment heads of nations the supreme capacity to achieve the destinies of nations without forcing upon them as a price, the mutilation and death of millions of citizens.

Resort to force in the Great War failed to bring tranquility. Victory and defeat were alike sterile. That lesson the world should have learned. For that reason above all others I addressed on September 26 my appeal to Your Excellency and to the President of Czechoslovakia and to the Prime Ministers of Great Britain and of France.

The two points I sought to emphasize were, first, that all matters of difference between the German Government and the Czechoslovak Government could and should be settled by pacific methods; and, second, that the threatened alternative of the use of force on a scale likely to result in a general war is as unnecessary as it is unjustifiable. It is, therefore, supremely important that negotiations should continue without interruption until a fair and constructive solution is reached.

My conviction on these two points is deepened because responsible statesmen have officially stated that an agreement in principle has already been reached between the Government of the German Reich and the Government of Czechoslovakia, although the precise time, method and detail of carrying out that agreement remain an issue.

Whatever existing differences may be, and whatever their merits may be—and upon them I do not and need not undertake to pass—my appeal was solely that negotiations be continued until a peaceful settlement is found, and that thereby a resort to force be avoided.

Present negotiations still stand open. They can be continued if you give the word. Should the need for supplementing them become evident, nothing stands in the way of widening their scope into a conference of all the nations directly interested in the present controversy. Such a meeting to be held immediately—in some neutral spot in Europe—would offer the opportunity for this and correlated questions to be solved in a spirit of justice, of fair dealing, and, in all human probability, with greater permanence.

In my considered judgment, and in the light of the experience of this century, continued negotiations remain the only way by which the immediate problem can be disposed of upon any lasting basis.

Should you agree to a solution in this peaceful manner I am convinced that hundreds of millions throughout the world would recognize your action as an outstanding historic service to all humanity.

Allow me to state my unqualified conviction that history, and the souls of every man, woman, and child whose lives will be lost in the threatened war will hold us and all of us accountable should we omit any appeal for its prevention.

The Government of the United States has no political involvements in Europe, and will assume no obligations in the conduct of the present negotiation. Yet in our own right we recognize our responsibilities as a part of a world of neighbors.

The conscience and the impelling desire of the people of my country demand that the voice of their government be raised again and yet again to avert and to avoid war.

This message was sent at 10:18 P.M.

Mr. Marburg was deeply concerned with the trend of events,

especially during 1938 and the early part of 1939. He protested vigorously against the ineffective policy of neutrality saying:

Objections to the embargo, misnamed neutrality, may be said to rest on a few plain facts.

It cannot be effective unless all or nearly all the trading countries support it. Failing that essential, the countries remaining out will serve as gateways through which supplies will still pass to the offender.

It operates unevenly. The British Isles have a seven weeks' food supply. Let an international embargo be placed on shipments to them and they would soon be starved into submission. Apply, for a like offense, the same embargo against the United States, and our abundant home supplies would cause us to feel hunger pressure not at all.

Especially stupid is isolated action in this field. By blocking our own exports while leaving other lands free to trade with the offender we starve masses of industrial workers at home and not only leave quantities of farm products unsold, but, by increasing the surplus, lower the price of that which can still be sold at home.

Our present neutrality law penalizes both the innocent and the guilty. In the cause of world order we should help the innocent and punish only the guilty by economic measures. But how? Of the two, the country with the stronger fleet can, by paying for it, legally appropriate all we seek to send to the other. The inescapable conclusion is that, in the international field, economic penalties, whether labeled embargo, boycott or neutrality, are half measures which deter none and do more harm than good.

Mr. Marburg also questioned the Government's attitude on

the tariff issue. He recognized that trade between the nations is one of the most important and dangerous questions to be faced. Channels of trade must be kept open but also the highway must be a "two lane road." The buying nation must also sell or it cannot pay for the goods it buys. He asked:

If present methods are open to criticism, what, then, can be done to correct world conditions? The chief need is for a general sense of political security under which economic conditions would gradually right themselves and extreme nationalism disappear. This sense of security it is in the power of the United States to provide by joining the League of Nations and accepting its share of responsibility under it. We could enter the League by joint resolution of the Congress, the method followed recently in getting us into the International Labor Office and previously in acquiring Texas and Hawaii after the Senate had turned down treaties for their annexation.

He was sure in his own mind that if we joined the League even at this late date our assumption of responsibilities would very likely influence Germany and Italy to change their attitude toward the world organization.

With all the Western nations, including ourselves, as members the word of the League would have real authority. It would then be possible to revive all the original powers of the covenant, especially that which makes the recalcitrant the common enemy and add the positive obligation of the Geneva Protocol of 1924, the obligation to use military force against the aggressor. The object of the criminal law is prevention, not revenge. That principle should also hold good in the application of international law. Nothing will actually prevent wars except the knowledge beforehand that a united world will make war on the aggressor.

Although Germany and Italy carried on the war, and eventually included Japan as an Axis Power, it became clear that the principal drive was in Berlin—not in Rome or Tokyo. Japan's attack on Pearl Harbor brought us into the war, and from that time on a series of meetings were held here in support of the war effort. Mr. Marburg spoke often and he always came back to the one point that he had stressed strongly during and before the war —and even during World War I, i.e., the chief responsibility for the conflict rested upon Germany. Marburg was called on for various services. He made speeches constantly. In one of his best thought-out statements he developed the thesis that all the trouble in Germany stemmed from the day under Bismarck when Germany became a united power under the domination and control of Prussia. One of his most drastic suggestions was that "when the war has been won—and I have no doubt of the outcome— the tie between the German states should be dissolved and each state should become an independent unit; and that Prussia should be quarantined until she is cured of the virus that has affected all the German states and brought on two world wars."

CHAPTER TWELVE

The United Nations

That Peace Bird Is Getting Popular

CHAPTER TWELVE

The United Nations

IN AN ADDRESS IN Portland, Oregon, September 15, 1919, President Wilson said: "The whole trouble about our civilization, as it looks to me, is that it has grown complex faster than we have adjusted the simpler ideas to the existing conditions." Then he illustrated the point by showing how, although we had come to rely upon each other more and more, we had not, at the same time, found any adequate way by which we could solve our larger difficulties. Continuing, he said: "Whether you will or not, our fortunes are tied up with the rest of the world and the choice we have made now is whether or not we will accept the influences of the rest of the world and be affected by them, or dominate these influences and lead them."

In another address, delivered during this same fateful campaign, which he made in behalf of the League of Nations, he warned the country that if the United States refused to enter the world organization, the League would fail and there would follow, as the judgment of "a vengeful god," a war more devastating than mankind had ever known. In this speech, he spoke with the zeal and with the flaming words of the ancient prophets of Israel. Unfortunately, our nation and its leaders did not listen. In fact, in many circles today, Woodrow Wilson is blamed for having destroyed his own League, whereas, what he said regarding the League, particularly when staunch friends of it went back on their own creation, was: "The League that has been defeated is not the League set up by the Peace Conference but an instrument that will, from its very inception, be incapable of carrying out the high purposes assigned to it in the covenant."

Theodore Marburg recognized a similar fact, that the League, without the United States, could not fulfill its destiny. He saw, with regret, the widening gaps in its structure. But most of all, he expressed his regret, time and time again, at the callous attitude taken by the United States in those years so filled with fate for the future.

A parallel might even be drawn between conditions in the 1920's and what is going on in the world at the present time. President Woodrow Wilson, who had not only been the founder of the League but was a great analyst of history, pointed out the role that the new Russia would probably play.

The Russian revolution, he noted, which ended with the destruction of the Czarist system, brought Russian Bolshevism, with its communist philosophy, into the world picture, its opening phase being an attack on capitalism. It was inevitable, therefore, that the new Russia should take Marx seriously. The Bolsheviks were soon playing the game of politics at home so effectively that it was not long before they were able to create serious discord in other countries. The Russian people, however, as a whole, knew little or nothing of diplomatic matters and had little facility in the management of their own affairs. They were ruled by a small coterie of men who, while professing democratic ideals, were solidly opposed to taking the people into their confidence. It was impossible for any one of the "proletariat" to learn the true facts of what was going on in the minds of the men behind the walls of the Kremlin.

World trade is another factor that complicates matters in dealing with Russia. The lifeblood of the nations is international trade; but when the Russian State took over all industry she abolished individual initiative and ownership. She, therefore, has no domestic competition. The state pays and controls the workers. All profits above the cost of production go to the Government. Russia, by these means, is able to outsell any of the other nations in the world market. Because of her vast areas rich in food products and manpower, together with her mineral resources, forests and other supplies of raw materials, she is able to live almost in seclusion from the rest of the world. Nevertheless, there came a time, during World War II, when she needed outside assistance for the continuance of the struggle against the military prowess of Nazi Germany.

Early in August 1941, a number of battleships met in the North Atlantic, off the coast of Newfoundland. These vessels came not as belligerents, each hoping to destroy, but for the purpose of bringing closer together two of the most powerful nations on earth in a union against Germany and her allies. At this meeting, Mr. Churchill and President Roosevelt formulated a document which became known as the "Atlantic Charter." This was, in effect, a declaration of certain principles and aims to be achieved by the defeat of the Axis Powers in the war that had been raging for almost two years. We were not a belligerent nation at that time. The action which precipitated the United States into the war was the attack on Hawaii in December 1941, four months after the Atlantic Charter had been signed.

The Atlantic Charter laid the foundation stone for a new coalition of the nations which eventually became known as the United Nations. From this time on, other momentous conferences were held.

1. International Conferences:

Casablanca Conference. Held in January 1942. Agreement on the unconditional surrender of Germany and her allies. Moscow Conference. Held in October 1943. Agreement for World Organization.

Cairo Conference. Held in November 1943. Discussion: China and Cooperation; the Big Five.

Teheran Conference. Held in December 1943. Agreement on plans to finish the war.

Yalta Conference. Held in November 1944. Discussion of the future of Europe and the projected San Francisco Conference.

2. In addition to these international meetings, there were five conferences held in the United States:

Hot Springs, Virginia, Conference. Held in January 1943. Subject: Food and Nutrition.

Atlantic City Conference. Held in November 1943. Subject: Relief and Rehabilitation.

Philadelphia Conference. Held in April 1944. Subject: World Charter for Labor.

Bretton Woods Conference. Held in July 1944. Subject: International Bank and Finance.

Chicago—Air Conference. Held in December 1944. Subject: International Air Lines and Travel.

3. In addition, there was a Conference held in Dumbarton Oaks, near Washington, D.C., October 1944. Here, detailed plans for a World Organization were formulated. In fact, this Conference arranged the agenda which was later used as a basis for the San Francisco Conference, during which the United Nations was born. "The League is dead, long live the League."

The details in the preceding paragraphs must be kept in mind if one is to understand clearly that the supreme purpose in the minds of the political leaders among the allies was two-fold: first, to win the war and, second, to establish a world organization which would, through the creating of a general community of interest, render itself capable of bringing about the abolition of war by adjustment through peaceful means of disputes between the nations.

Mr. Marburg wrote in "World Affairs," December 1944, an article in which he heartily approved of the efforts which had been made to establish the new world organization. In part, he said:

> Obstruction, both in the adoption and, later, in the application of the Dumbarton Oaks Proposals may be looked for from certain quarters, but the problem of devising a sound plan is a simple one. In 1923, Geneva framed the 'Treaty of Mutual Assistance.' This was perfected the following year as the 'Geneva Protocol' and adopted unanimously by all the States represented. It obligated the States members of the League to use force forthwith to punish the aggressor, the plan of the old American League to Enforce Peace. The 'Geneva Protocol' was adopted by the League of Nations while the Labor Government was in the saddle in Great Britain. When the Conservatives turned out McDonald, Austin Chamberlain promptly shelved the measure.

> We already have close cooperation of the English-speaking peoples. All that is needed is to preserve that union after the war, preferably in the form of actual Federation, and supplement it by a revived League of Nations fortified with the Geneva Protocol of 1924.

> We have the authority of William Howard Taft for the assertion that, inasmuch as the treaty-making power of the United States extends to all subjects usually dealt with in treaties, it follows that we have the right to agree to submission of future disputes for peaceful settlement.

> The serious defect of the proposals of the Dumbarton Oaks

Conference is the failure to provide that the vote of the state accused of aggression shall not operate to veto a resolution of the governing body.

Thus, Mr. Marburg foresaw some of the problems the United Nations faces today, such as the use and misuse of the veto and the question how, when and where armed forces shall be used, and by whom and under what circumstances. The answers are given in the Charter of the United Nations. The provision regarding the veto was written into the Charter at the insistance of the American delegation. Without the veto, the Security Council of the United Nations might become an instrument of tyranny. In San Francisco, when the matter was being discussed, those who opposed acceptance of the veto emphasized the fact that the right to veto can only be exercised by the five great powers: Britain, America, France, Russia and China. These critics asked, and the question was repeated all over the city: "If these five are the cops and one of *them* becomes an aggressor, who will cop the cop?"

The United Nations is a much stronger and more effective organization than the League of Nations and the establishment of an International Police Force is being studied, but it will have to be worked out gradually, with great patience and care. At the same time, the United Nations stresses its faith in democracy in the preamble to its Covenant which reads:

The peoples of the United Nations determined to save succeeding generations from the scourge of war, which twice in our lifetime has brought untold sorrow to mankind, and to reaffirm faith in fundamental human rights, in the dignity and worth of the human person, in the equal rights of men and women and of nations large and small, and to establish conditions under which justice and respect for the obligations arising from treaties and other sources of international law can be maintained, and to promote social progress and better standards of life in larger freedom, and for these ends to practice tolerance and live together in peace with one another as good neighbors, and to unite our strength to maintain international peace and security, and to ensure, by the acceptance of principles and the institution of methods, that armed force shall not be used, save in the common interest, and to employ international machinery for the promotion of the economic and social advancement of all peoples.

After five years, the United Nations has proved itself to be a most valuable and effective organization. Of course, we must recognize it is not perfect, but it is capable of being perfected. It has achieved a measure of success and is now recognized throughout the world as the "one best hope for peace in our time." Its sole purpose is, after all, to establish and maintain the peace of the world. With this achieved, all other things can be added as extra dividends for the good of mankind. As a machine, its work will be no better than the men, women and nations working with it. The hesitant attitudes of nations to accept the authority of the organization grows out of an over-emphasis on sovereignty. A nation that asserts its rights, regardless of rights and privileges of other nations, proves itself a bad neighbor. The United Nations' concept of the community is based on the religious principles of brotherhood, sacrifice and service. Just as a citizen of Baltimore is, at the same time, a citizen of Maryland and of the United States, so he is because of these relationships also a citizen of the world. No one can resign from the human race. The earth is the common home of all people. We accept our responsibility as citizens of the community, and live in accord with certain principles of right and wrong. Each person is either good or bad according to his attitude toward his neighbor, and the degree with which he respects and obeys the laws of the community. The United Nations is a prototype of the world community to be. World citizenship, in the real sense, is still only a dream—but a dream that will be one day realized. All the states represented in the United Nations are committed to the development of a great world community. Our own country by its membership in the United Nations is obligated to practice, as far as possible, the universal, moral and ethical principles of fair dealing and right relations with all nations. No nation can live to itself, anymore than an individual can live his life without recognizing his responsibility to his neighbor. It is, therefore, incumbent upon the citizens of all countries to urge their governments to utilize the machinery of the United Nations as far as possible. Without being overly critical, it is true that our own government has, in too many instances, ignored the United Nations by carrying out its own plans without first referring such actions to the world organization.

The success of the United Nations rests upon the ability with which the nations will avail themselves of the machinery they have helped to create. The machine can be made more perfect only through use. The United Nations is a worthy successor of the League of Nations and vindicates the thought and aspirations of Theodore Marburg and his associates who believed thoroughly that there is enough intelligence and goodwill in the world to help save us from the catastrophe of a new war. This can be done and we can save ourselves and our civilization if we are willing to pay the price, giving up some of our prerogatives, and work wholeheartedly with men and women, even with those with whom we differ. The ability to live together in peace with a neighbor is the test of the democratic way of life.

Theodore Marburg, in an article published in the *Baltimore Sun* in 1912, noted some of the dangers that have always faced democracy:

At the outset, let me profess my faith in representative democracy and confidence in the united thinking of the many. The great fact of the past has been the oppression of the many by the few. Unless we have democracy, violent revolution is required to throw off the oppressive rule of the few. This is the justification of democracy and a sufficient reason for its existence as a permanent and not a passing phase of political development.

Moreover, the united thinking of the many results in thinking true. The few have generally led throughout history, either to the advantage or disadvantage of the many. But when it comes to sound thinking, just as the united judgment of a jury of twelve men on a question of fact is superior to that of any one man, so the judgment of the people as a whole is superior to that of any small group. But it is essential that democracy should be representative and that the will of the people should be the *informed* will of the people, which is the result of real thinking.

Our Republic has lasted longer than any important republic in history. What explains it? To my mind, it is due principally to two things—representative government and local government for local affairs. So long as the local government exists, extent of dominion does not endanger the life of a republic; so long as representative government exists, there is a chance of escaping the tyrannical action of the majority which characterized ancient democracies.

In another article, he stresses another category of the questions which are again being discussed today.

Our present institutions, local and national, are sound. It is their operation that is faulty, due solely to our neglect. The men who set up these institutions were closer to the times of license, the license of the powerful and the license of the mob.

It was to guard against both that they planned, because both are equally enemies of liberty.

You will remember how the practice of ostracism often banished the Athenian citizen from his beloved Attica without rhyme or reason. His very virtues may have made enemies among the populace, and if numerous enough they banished him by vote. You will remember the awkward habit acquired by Roman emperors of sending word to some individual that his room on earth was more desired than his company and of inviting the gentleman to open his veins. The victim sometimes gathered his friends around him in a brilliant farewell banquet and, amid such a scene, obeyed the emperor. But, whether ending his days thus in the manner of the dying swan or, like a rat caught in a trap and drowned, the fact was that when he got such a command, he always did proceed to open his veins, because he knew that if he failed to do it a more terrible end awaited him. The Roman dominion was the civilized world. There was no place to which he could flee, bearable for a civilized man to live in, where the arm of Rome could not reach him.

You will remember how accusations dropped into the lion's mouth at Venice resulted in men being whisked off to the star chamber for secret trial and conducted thence across the Bridge of Sighs to prison. You will remember how, under the old regime in France, a *lettre de cachet,* secured from some private enemy who had influence at court, sufficed to take a man for the remainder of his life to the dungeons of the Bastile, where often even his identity was unknown to the keeper. Our freedom and the freedom of the world are worth guarding against encroachments of all kinds.

The people in all nations want peace. Peace can be established only by the expenditure of an almost incredible amount of good will and forebearance by all parties and groups in all nations. The churches and religious organizations have a most important part to play in creating that required good will.

His views on "the church as a League for Peace" were published in the *Baltimore Sun,* August 18, 1927:

The object of this letter is not to try to strengthen the argument but to express the hope that the matter will not be allowed to sleep; that it will be taken up seriously and persistently until the suggestion is realized.

The aim is humanitarian, not exclusively religious, and there is nothing to prevent the realization of the proposal that the Roman Catholic Church head the movement, loath as that church is to cooperate with Protestant denominations in reliligious matters.

In this case, its cooperation, in fact, leadership is essential. The late Cardinal Gibbons was ever ready to lend his name and give his active support to humanitarian movements, irrespective of the religious persuasion of the persons who were affiliated.

If war comes, I fear all ties—class, family, religion—will melt away in the burning fire of patriotism, well or ill directed. But a church united for peace and organized to help along practical plans and institutions to avoid war would be of greatest value.

Since this was written the churches and religious-minded people have accepted a larger responsibility than ever for world affairs. Members of churches, temples and synagogues are constantly urging their people to cooperate with other groups in the community in support of the United Nations. They are enlightening as well as leading their people in programs of study and action. The churches of America agree with the vast majority of our citizens in support of the use of force to maintain our security and to help meet our commitments to the United Nations. At the same time it is firmly believed that armed force alone is not enough. The indiscriminate use of the hydrogen and atomic bombs, bacteria, and other devilish instruments can never prevent war and can never win a war—but can only help to bring about the complete demotilion of what is left of our sadly torn and suffering civilization.

The first building on the grounds of the permanent home of the United Nations in New York City is now completed. It is forty-one stories high—a most imposing monument to the hopes and ideals of people all over the world. In this building will be housed the secretariat of the United Nations with some two thousand workers, representatives of sixty nations. They will talk of many things in many tongues. In fact, nearly every language spoken in the civilized world will be heard in its halls and offices. This building, standing as a tower, is also a symbol. Will it be a Tower of Babel, in which confusion of tongues, ill will, disagrement on policy, and frustration will bring the structure down in ruins? Or will it be a "lighthouse," guiding past dangers and at the same time promising hope and security as we try to find our way through the mist and fog of the world's present uncertainty and disappointment?

The answer to these questions can be given only by the people themselves. "Wars begin in the minds of men," and peace can be assured only by convincing a majority of the people in all lands that they can have peace if they are willing to work to secure it.

The American Association for the United Nations is making a diligent effort to win the American public to this point of view. This organization, which began its existence as a supporter of the League of Nations twenty-seven years ago, commenced its support of the United Nations even before the charter of the world organization was adopted. Before the end of World War II an influential group, led by Dr. James T. Shotwell, Mr. Malcolm W. Davis, Mr. Clark M. Eichelberger, and Colonel Charles L. Marburg, formulated a program, which has through national and local leadership won a large following in the United States. The Association maintains an active national headquarters in New York with twelve regional offices and fifty state and local groups. It also took a leading part in forming the "World Federation of United Nations Associations," which now has some fifty national branches working together to secure universal support of the United Nations as the keystone in the foreign policy of all nations.

Mr. Marburg was true to his ideals. He worked hard for the League to Enforce Peace and the League of Nations, and lived long enough to see established a newer and more perfect world organization of his dreams. If the United Nations is given the opportunity, and the nations and their people will turn aside from their prejudices and wholeheartedly support this embryonic world community, it will grow and become strong. The United Nations can help to bring about that day toward which man has looked for more than six thousand years—the day when swords are beaten into plowshares and spears into pruning hooks. Then "nation shall not lift up sword against nation, neither shall they learn war anymore."

Theodore Marburg will be long remembered because of himself and what he was, his heroic spirit, courage, downrightness, and his efforts to help build a saner, safer and better world order.

BIBLIOGRAPHY

of works by Theodore Marburg

The World's Money Problem. Cushing & Co., Baltimore. 1896.

Political Papers. J. Murphy & Co., Baltimore. 1898. (Reprinted from The Baltimore American.)

Political Papers: Expansion. J. Murphy & Co. 1900. (Reprinted from The American.)

The Municipal Art Society: Its Activities, Aims and Hopes. An address ai Johns Hopkins University, January 8, 1902.

Do We Want An Asset Currency? Address delivered before the National Civic Federation, New York, December 16, 1907. Published 1908.

The Panic and the Present Depression. Address delivered before the American Academy of Political and Social Science, Philadelphia, 1908.

The American Society for the Judicial Settlement of International Disputes. Baltimore, 1910.

A Few Considerations on the Settlement of International Disputes by Means Other Than War. Philadelphia, 1910.

The Peace Movement Practical. Maryland Peace Society, 1910. Maryland Quarterly, November 1910, No. 4.

Philosophy of the Third American Peace Congress. (Pamphlet.) May, 1912.

Law and Judicial Settlement. (Pamphlet.) 1915. Quoted from it: "In The Hague Convention governing the establishment of the Court there is nothing which can be interpreted as requiring concerted action on the part of all the powers."

The League of Nations Should Be Formed Immediately. Article in the "Humanitarian," December 1918.

League of Nations. Macmillan & Company, New York. 1918.

Draft Convention for League of Nations, by group of American jurists and publicists. Description and comment by Theodore Marburg. Macmillan & Co., 1918.

In the Hills (Poems). G. P. Putnam Sons, New York. 1924.

Bobbylinkapoo (Poem for children). Dorrance & Co., Philadelphia. 1931.

Development of the League of Nations Idea. Edited by John Latane. Two Volumes. Macmillan & Co. 1932.

The Story of a Soul. Dorrance & Co. 1938. (Based on *Life of Marie Adelaide, Granduchess of Luxembourg,* by Edith O'Shaughnessy, and an official proceedings of the Luxembourg Parliament.